Blades of Glory
Epic Battles of the
MARATHA EMPIRE

Vyankatesh Desai

HAWK PRESS

Published by

Hawk Press
4836/24, Ansari Road, Daryaganj
New Delhi – 110 002
Phones : 9643330713, +91-11-23278618, +91-11-35676207
E-mail : thehawkpress@gmail.com
www.thehawkpress.com

CONTENTS

CHAPTER 1

Introduction

The Maratha Conquests were a series of conquests in the Indian subcontinent which led to the building of the Maratha Empire.

These conquests were started by Shivaji in 1659 from the victory at the Battle of Pratapgad against Bijapur. The expansion of the empire was limited and interrupted by the Mughal conquests of south India by Mughal emperor Aurangzeb. Marathas were forced to defend their territories against the overwhelmingly strong Mughal army in the 27 years long Deccan wars.

They were able to defend their territories and gain an upper hand over Mughals in the sustained conflict.

Afterwards, the Marathas conclusively defeated and overtook major territories of the Mughal Empire in the Indian subcontinent and its vassals.

It ended with the eventual fall of the Maratha Empire after the Anglo-Maratha Wars.

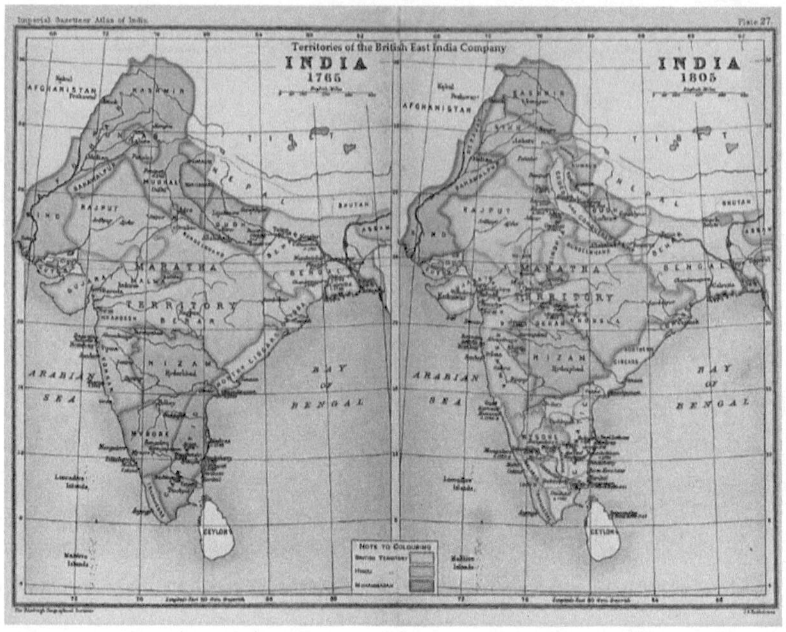

Map of India, comparing 1765 and 1805

List of Battles fought by Chhatrapati Shivaji Maharaj

Shivaji's father Shahji had earlier served as a Jagirdar under Adil Shah. Shivaji inherited this land and later revolted against the Adil Shahi dynasty, carving out a kingdom with Raigad as his capital. After Treaty of Purandar signed on 11 June 1665, Shivaji was incorporated as a vassal and had to send his son Sambhaji to fight for the Mughals in the Deccan as a mansabdar along with 5,000 horsemen, Shivaji seeing that he wasn't getting much prestige in Mughal Darbar, revolted and fought against the Mughals and raided the rich city of Surat.

He crowned himself in 1674 as a Chhatrapati, establishing the Maratha Kingdom Shivaji died in 1680. After Shivaji Maharaj, Sambhaji took up throne. He built strong army as well as navy. Mughal emperor Aurangzeb shifted his capital from Delhi to Aurangabad to defeat Sambhaji. The Mughals invaded, fighting an War of 27 years from 1681 to 1707 in which the Marathas under Tarabai were victorious. Sambhaji was captured during this war and killed by Mughals. Shahu I, a grandson of Shivaji, ruled as emperor until 1749. During his reign, Shahu appointed the first Peshwa as head of the government, under certain conditions. After the death of Shahu, the Peshwas became the de facto leaders of the Empire from 1749 to 1761, while Shivaji's successors continued as nominal rulers from their base in Satara. Covering a major part of the subcontinent, the Maratha Empire kept the British forces at bay during the 18th century, until internal relations between the Peshwas and their sardars (army commanders) deteriorated, provoking its gradual downfall.

The Maratha Empire was at its height in the 18th century under Shahu and the Peshwa Baji Rao I. Losses at the Third Battle of Panipat in 1761 suspended further expansion of the empire in the North-west and reduced the power of the Peshwas.

In 1761, after severe losses in the Panipat war, the Peshwas slowly started losing the control of the kingdom. Many military chiefs of Maratha Empire like Shinde, Holkar, Gaikwad, Pant Pratinidhi, Bhosale of Nagpur, Dev (Gade) of Wardha, Pandit of Bhor, Patwardhan, and Newalkar started to work towards their ambition of becoming kings in their respective regions. However, under Madhavrao Peshwa, Maratha authority in North India was restored, 10 years after the battle of Panipat. After the death of Madhavrao, the empire gave way to a loose Confederacy, with political power resting in a 'pentarchy' of five mostly Maratha dynasties: the Peshwas of Pune; the Sindhias (originally "Shindes") of Malwa and Gwalior; the Holkars of Indore; the Bhonsles of Nagpur; and the Gaekwads of Baroda. A rivalry between the Sindhia and Holkar dominated the confederation's affairs into the early 19th century, as did the clashes with the British and the British East India Company in the three Anglo-Maratha Wars.

In the Third Anglo-Maratha War, the last Peshwa, Baji Rao II, was defeated by the British in 1818 and the empire ceased to exist.

2.1 Battle of Pratapgarh

The fort of Pratapgad

The Battle of Pratapgad was a battle fought on 10 November 1659 at the fort of Pratapgad near the town of Satara, Maharashtra, India between the forces of the Marathas under Shivaji and the Adilshahi troops under the Adilshahi general Afzal Khan. The Marathas defeated the Adilshahi forces. It was their first significant military victory against a major regional power.

2.1.1 Background

Shivaji held a commendable position in parts of Maval. The Adilshahi court wanted to curb his activities. Afzal Khan, a renowned general of Bijapur who had previously killed Shivaji's elder brother Sambhaji in a battle, was selected to lead an assault against Shivaji. He started from Bijapur in 1659. Shivaji met Afzal

Khan on 10 November 1659 and killed him in a truce negotiation. Shivaji's forces then routed the scattered Adilshahi army.

2.1.2 Combat of Shivaji and Afzal Khan

Shivaji sent an emissary to Afzal Khan, stating that he did not want to fight and was ready for peace. A meeting was arranged between Shivaji and Afzal Khan at a shamiyana (highly decorated tent) at the foothills of Pratapgad. It was agreed that they would each bring only ten personal bodyguards with them. All the ten bodyguards would remain 'one arrow-shot' away from the pair. Shivaji chose Sambhaji Kondhalkar, Jiva Mahala, Siddi Ibrahim, Kataji Ingle, Kondaji Kank, Yesaji Kank, Krishnaji Gaikwad, Surji Katake, Visaji Murambak & Sambhaji Karvar for the meet. Afzal Khan hid a katyar (a small dagger) in his coat, and Shivaji wore armour underneath his clothes and carried a concealed *wagh nakha* in one hand.

As the two men entered the tent, the 6'7" tall Afzal Khan embraced Shivaji. He then tried to strangle Shivaji in his vice-like grip and pierced his dagger in Shivaji. But the armour under Shivaji's clothes saved him. Shivaji retaliated by using his "wagh nakh" (tiger claws) to slash Khan's stomach and disemboweled Khan. Thereupon, Afzal Khan's bodyguard Bada Sayyed attacked Shivaji with a sword but Shivaji's personal bodyguard, Jiva Mahala, fatally struck him down. Also the lawyer of Afzal Khan, Krishna Bhaskar Kulkarni attacked Shivaji. Shivaji killed Krishna Kulkarni with his sword. Afzal Khan managed to hold his gushing entrails and hurtled, fainting and bleeding, outside the tent and threw himself into his palanquin. The bearers hastily lifted their charge and began moving rapidly away down the slope. Sambhaji Kavji Kondhalkar, Shivaji's lieutenant and one of the accompanying guards, gave chase and beheaded Afzal Khan. The severed head was later sent to Rajgad to be shown to Shivaji's mother, Jijabai. She had long wanted vengeance for the deliberate maltreatment of Shahaji (Shivaji's father) while a captive of Afzal Khan, and for his role in the death of her elder son, Sambhaji Shahaji Raje Bhosle. Shivaji sped up the slope towards the fortress and his lieutenants ordered cannons to be fired. It was a signal to his infantry, hidden in the densely forested valley, to raid the Adilshahi forces.

2.1.3 Hand-to-hand combat of the forces

Maratha troops commanded by Shivaji's captain Kanhoji Jedhe, swept down on Afzal Khan's 1,500 soldiers; resulting in a complete rout at the foothills of the fort. Then in a rapid march, a section of Adilshahi forces commanded by Musekhan was attacked. Musekhan, Afzal Khan's lieutenant, was wounded and subsequently fled the field.

Meanwhile, Moropant Pingle led the Maratha infantry toward the left flank of Adilshahi troops. The suddenness of this attack on Afzal Khan's artillery at close quarters made them ineffective in providing artillery cover for the main portion of their troops. And as a result of this the rest of their troops rapidly succumbed to an all out Maratha attack. Simultaneously Shivaji's Sardar (captain), Ragho Atre's cavalry units swooped down and attacked the large but unprepared Adilshahi cavalry before they were able to be fully geared up for battle and succeeded in completely routing them in short order.

The Maratha cavalry under Netaji Palkar pursued the retreating Adilshahi forces, who were attempting to join up with the part of their reserve forces stationed in the nearby village of Wai. They were engaged in battle before they could regroup and were defeated prior to reaching Wai. The Adilshahi forces not withstanding the onslaught of the Marathas started retreating towards Bijapur. The Maratha army chased the retreating army and on their way captured 23 Adilshahi forts. In fact, the Adilshahi *Killedar* of the Kolhapur fort himself handed over the keys to the Marathas.

2.1.4 Aftermath

Adilshahi forces lost their artillery, 65 elephants, 4000 horses, 1200 camels, jewels worth 300,000 Rupees, 1,000,000 Rupees, heaps of precious clothes and tents to the Marathas. They also lost their money and grain stored at Wai.

5,000 Adilshahi soldiers were killed and many others were wounded. 3,000 soldiers were imprisoned, and the remainder were allowed to go home in defeat. The Marathas lost 1,734 soldiers, while 420 soldiers were wounded.

As it was the policy of Shivaji to humanely treat the defeated army, neither the men nor women were sold as slaves or molested. Wounded commanders were offered treatment deserving of their rank and either imprisoned or sent back to Bijapur. Some of the defeated Adilshahi generals like Siddi Hilal changed their loyalties and joined the Marathas to serve under Shivaji. Two of Afzal Khan's sons were captured by the Marathas but were let off by the Shivaji. Fazal khan (son of Afzal Khan) and the Adilshahi soldiers with him who were badly injured were shown a safe passage out of the forest of Jawli by Prataprao More. Shivaji also buried Afzal Khan as per Islamic customs and built his tomb near Pratapgarh, as per his philosophy of 'once the enemy is dead, the enmity is dead too'.

The sword of honour was presented to Kanhoji Jedhe for his invaluable and outstanding performance of service to Shivaji. The relatives of the killed soldiers were offered service in the Maratha army. Families without any male left alive to support, the family were awarded pensions. Heroes of the war were rewarded with medals, kada (bracelets) and horses.

Khan's death dealt the Adilshah's rule a severe blow. A quarter of his territory, forts and a fifth of his army were captured or destroyed, while Shivaji doubled his territory, losing a tenth of his army, within fifteen days of the Battle of Pratapgadh. Shivaji maintained his momentum, sending cavalry towards Kolhapur, which succeeded in capturing seventeen forts, including the prestigious fort of Panhala. Cavalry was also sent towards Dabhol and Rajapur under the command of Doroji Patil, which was successful in capturing forts in the southern Konkan.

This remarkable victory made Shivaji a hero of Maratha folklore and a legendary figure among his people. Having established military dominance and successfully beaten back a major attack by a powerful empire, Shivaji had founded the nucleus of what would become the Maratha Empire.

2.2 Battle of Kolhapur

Battle of Kolhapur was a battle that took place on 28 December 1659 near the city of Kolhapur, Maharashtra between the Shivaji and the Adilshahi forces. The battle is known for brilliant movement of flanks by Shivaji, similar to tactics of Babur against Rana Sanga.

2.2.1 Background

Shivaji had killed Afzal Khan and routed his army in the battle of Pratapgarh on 10 November 1659. He took advantage of this victory and in a great offensive took a large hilly tract running about 200 km under his command. A number of forts like Vasota fell to Marathas. By December 1659, Shivaji appeared near Panhala fort. Rustam Zaman was directed from Bijapur. He arrived near Miraj in the vicinity of Kolhapur on 27 December 1659.

2.2.2 Battle

2.2.2.1 Composition of Adilshah's forces

Rustam Zaman was assisted by other chieftains: Fazal Khan, Malik Itbar, Sadat Khan, Yakub Khan, Aankush Khan, Hasan Khan, Mulla Yahya and Santaji Ghatage. Adilshah's forces were consisted of selected well known cavalry. In addition, elephants were deployed as first line of defense. The centre was commanded by Rustam Zaman himself, left flank by Fazal Khan, right flank by Malik Itbar. Fateh Khan and Mullah Yahya were on the rear guard. In total Rustam Zaman had an army of 10,000 cavalry.

2.2.2.2 Composition of Maratha forces

Shivaji was assisted by Maratha Cavalry leaders: Netaji Palkar, Sardar Godaji Jagtap, Hiroji Ingale, Bhimaji Wagh, Sidhoji Pawar Jadhavrao, Hanmantrao Kharate, Pandhare, Siddi Hllal, and Mahadik. Center was commanded by Shivaji himself. Siddi Hilal and Jadhavrao were on left flank. Ingale and Sidhoji Pawar on right flank. Mahadik and Wagh on the rear guard. Netaji Palkar was off the centre. In all Shivaji commanded an army of 3,500 light cavalry much less than his rival Rustam's 10,000 cavalry.

2.2.2.3 Movement and clash of forces

Rustam Zaman was planning to move towards Panhala fort. Shivaji anticipated this movement and in a quick dash, with 3,500 cavalry appeared before the 10,000 strong Adilshahi forces and attacked the enemy in the early morning of 28 December 1659. Shivaji charged the center and instructed his generals to outflank the enemy. Other Maratha commanders attacked their respective flanks, resulting in 2,000 of Rustam Zaman force to be killed. With 20% of their army dead, and Shivaji pressing hard from the center, Rustam's forces started to crumble and ran away from the battle. By afternoon Rustam Zaman had fled the field.

2.2.3 Outcome

Shivaji gained a large territory and secured front of his emerging empire. Adilshahi forces lost about 2000 horses and 12 elephants to the Marathas. The Marathas under Shivaji's leadership, continued to conquer more Adilshahi territories. In one of the incidences, Shivaji tried to conquer an Adilshahi fort named *Khelna* but the terrain of the fort was difficult; conquering the fort was easier said than done. The Adilshahi garrison at the fort was also defending the fort valiantly. Therefore, Shivaji came up with a plan. Accordingly, a group of Marathas went up to the fort and convinced the Adilshahi chief (*killedar*) at the fort that they were not content with the rule of Shivaji and thus, had come to serve Adilshah. The Marathas were successful and the next day, they revolted and caused total chaos inside the fort. Simultaneously, Shivaji attacked the fort from outside and within no time captured the fort. Shivaji renamed the fort as Vishalgad.

2.3 Battle of Pavan Khind

A 20th century depiction by painter M.V. Dhurandhar of Shivaji and Baji Prabhu at Pawan Khind

Battle of Pävankhind was a rearguard last stand that took place on 13 July 1660, at a mountain pass in the vicinity of fort Vishalgad, near the city of Kolhapur, Maharashtra, India between the Maratha Warrior Baji Prabhu Deshpande, Sambhu Singh Jadhav and Siddi Masud of Adilshah Sultanate. The engagement ended with the destruction of the Maratha forces, and a tactical victory for the Bijapur Sultanate, but failing to achieve a strategic victory.

2.3.1 Background

In 1660, Shivaji was trapped in the fort of Panhala, under siege and vastly outnumbered by an Adilshahi army led by an Abyssinian named Siddi Masud. The ruler at the time was Ali Adil Shah II. Adilshahi, having suffered several defeats from Shivaji, and even though they were at odds with Mughals, had aligned with the Mughals to temper Shivaji's ambition. Baji Prabhu Deshpande managed to engage a large Adilshahi army with 300 soldiers in a rearguard action at the narrow pass of Ghod Khind, while Shivaji continued on to breech the siege at Vishal Gadh.

2.3.2 Prelude

Shivaji planned to escape to the fort of Vishalgadh, which was administered by a Maratha chieftain named Rango Narayan Orpe under Shivaji. Two Maratha sardars under the Adilshahi Commander Siddi Jouhar, namely Suryarao Surve and Jaswantrao Dalvi had also encircled the fort of Vishalgadh simultaneously. Shivaji waited for months, planning and depleting the Adilshah's food source. He waited until he reckoned that they needed to gather more food, and then started his plan.

Shivaji, Baji Prabhu, and around 600 of their best troops, hardened mountaineers of the Maval region, would dash through the Adilshahi force at night. A man named Shiva Kashid, who resembled Shivaji in appearance, had volunteered to dress like the king and get captured. It was envisaged that this would buy some additional time due to the confusion over identity, before Siddi Masud realised the error and gave chase.

Baji Prabhu Deshpande Statue in Panhala Fort

Shivaji made his escape on the dark night of 13 July, with his contingent of troops. Baji Prabhu was second in command of this contingent. The Adilshahis gave hot and rapid pursuit, with an army of 10,000. It was clear that there was no way to shake off the enemy, and that the Marathas would not simultaneously prevail over both the Moghul garrison at Vishagadh and the chasing Adilshahi army.

The only option was for a section of the Marathas to stay back and fight the larger Adilshahi forces in a rearguard action, while the rest of the Marathas would carry on to their destination. Shivaji decided that this was the inevitable choice and split his forces. Baji Prabhu Deshpande agreed to face the troops of Bijapur with 300 soldiers of the contingent. Shivaji told Baji Prabhu that he would hear the cannon fire from Vishalgadh (the destination fort), signalling Shivaji's safety. The strategic position of Ghod Khind (Horse Pass) was chosen for the defence. It was very narrow and only a few soldiers could pass at any one time.

2.3.3 Battle

Bajiprabhu Deshpande occupied Ghod Khind, blocking the path of the pursuers, and made a determined defence against them. His brother Fulaji Prabhu as well as sardars such as Shambusing Jadhav were present with him. Fulaji Prabhu and Shambusing were killed after a gallant and fierce fight. Baji Prabhu was severely wounded but carried on fighting at his station. The Adilshahi army repeatedly tried to break through the defenses of the pass, but were repeatedly repulsed. The unequal battle raged for hours, with the defenders maintaining their positions, but with rapidly depleting numbers. Only a handful of Marathas survived, and around a thousand soldiers of the Adilshahi army became casualties in attempting to take the pass.

Five hours after the battle started, the cannon fire announcing Shivaji's safe return to Vishalgadh was heard. Almost three hundred Marathas had been killed. Legend has it that a gravely injured Baji Prabhu continued engaging the enemy and held the pass, only laying down his life once he heard the sound of cannon fire. The handful surviving Marathas then retreated and disappeared in the forest as per the plan.

Shivaji and his 300 soldiers had to break through the encirclement of Suryarao and Jaswantrao at Vishalgadh. A fierce battle ensued in which Shivaji himself fought wearing Dandpatta in his both hands. Seeing this fight, the commander of Vishalgadh fort sent help to Shivaji enabling him and his troops to reach the fort safely. Shivaji then fired cannons as a signal for Baji Prabhu to retreat.

2.3.4 Aftermath

Shivaji's plan was successful. Having made his way to Vishalgadh, Rango Narayan Orpe had fresh troops at his disposal. Baji Prabhu had successfully fought the rearguard action and slowed the Adilshahis forces before they arrived at the fort having carried on pursuing Shivaji to Vishalgadh. The vengeful fresh Maratha troops carried out a blazing and bloody attack against Siddi Masood, Jasawantaro and Suryarao's forces inflicting heavy losses upon the latter when they arrived at the fort. The Adilshahi forces fled as a result of this attack. One Maratha chronicler describes this fierce attack by mentioning that the 'green valleys of Vishalgadh were painted in red due to enemy's blood'. Shivaji then safely crossed the western ghats and reached his capital Rajgad via Konkan region.

Shivaji later personally visited the house of the slain Baji Prabhu, which was in the village of Kasabe Sindh in the Raigad district and honoured his family, including giving his eldest son a position of leadership and honour in the forces.

The last stand, battle of Ghod Khind (Eng: Ghod pass) by about 300 Marathas led by the Baji Prabhu Deshpande was renamed "The Battle of Pavan Khind" which in Marathi means "The Battle of the Sacred Pass".

"The defence...," says historian Dennis Kincaid, "has become legendary in Western India. The action is remarkable as an example of the spirit which Chhatrapati Shivaji's leadership infused into his followers." Shivaji's mother, Jijabai, wept at the news of Baji Prabhu's death. Ballads and poems have been composed in his memory, some of which are still sung today. Sri Aurobindo, the great yogi, mystic and revolutionary of the 20th century wrote a poem dedicated to Baji Prabhu, which was used as a symbol to capture the spirit of sacrifice that was required of the young men in India's freedom struggle which was then under way.

Historian Jadunath Sarkar describes the incident in his book "Chhatrapati Shivaji and His Times" in the following way:

The siege dragged on for nearly four months; all the paths of ingress and egress were closed to the garrison. Shivaji found himself in a fatal trap. So, he wrote a secret letter to Jauhar, deceitfully begging his protection and offering to make an alliance with him. In order to negotiate for the terms he asked for a passport. Jauhar, "who was both fool and traitor," swallowed the bait; he assured Shivaji of his protection, gave him a safe conduct, and flattered himself that with Shiva for an ally he would be able to create a kingdom of his own in independence of Adil Shah. Next day Shivaji with only two or three followers visited Jauhar at midnight and was received in darbar. After oaths of co-operation had been taken on both sides, Shivaji returned quickly to the fort, and the pretended siege was continued. When the news of Jauhar's treacherous coquetting with Shiva reached the ears of Ali Adil Shah, that king burst into anger and left his capital (5 August) "to punish both the rebels." An envoy was sent to bring Jauhar back to the right path, but the mission was a failure. When, however, Ali reached Miraj and his Vanguard advanced beyond it still nearer to Panhala, Shivaji slipped out of the fort one night with his family and 2 to 3 hundred soldiers, and Panhala returned to Adil Shah's possession without a blow (about 25 August 1660.) As the Bijapur Court-poet sang in exultation, "Ali took Panhala from Salabat in a twinkle."

Shivaji's escape from the fort was soon detected, and a strong Bijapuri force under Jauhar's son Siddi Aziz and Afzal Khan's son Fazl Khan set out in pursuit of him. On reaching a narrow ravine (probably near Malkapur), Shiva left 300 men there under Baji Pradhu (the deshpande of Hardis Maval) with orders to hold the mouth of the pass at all costs till the main body of the fugitives had reached Vishalgad. The Bijapuris delivered three bloody assaults on the heroic rear-guard, all of which were beaten off. But when at last the gun-fire from Vishalgarh gave the anxiously expected signal that Shivaji had reached safety within its walls, the gallant Baji Prabhu was lying mortally wounded with 200 of his followers. Baji Prabhu had done his appointed duty. The Bijapuris declined to besiege Vishalgarh, and retired to their own territory, after recovering Pavangarh and some other forts in addition to Panhala. Shivaji retained in that quarter only the forts of Rangana and Vishalgarh.

2.4 Battle of Chakan

The Battle of Chakan was fought between the Marathas and the Mughal Empire in the year 1660. The Mughal army advancing towards Pune had to overcome the fort of Chakan around 30 km from the city.

The fort of Chakan was a *Bhuikot, i.e.* a land fort and was occupied by around 800 infantry. Mughal forces laid siege to the fort hoping for a quick surrender by the numerically inferior Maratha garrison. However the Mughal artillery was unable to force the fort into submission. Several assaults by the Mughals were repulsed with high casualties.

After almost two and half months without success the Mughals finally resorted to mining the *Buruj* or tower of the fort. With the towers demolished the Maratha force agreed to come to terms. The remainder of garrison withdrew from the fort.

2.4.1 Aftermath

The Mughal commander Shaista Khan was surprised with the prolonged resistance offered at the relatively small fort. The siege revealed glaring shortcomings of Mughal army like poor strategy and tactics and overconfidence. These were exploited by the Marathas when they routed a Mughal force deployed in Konkan, and again during the most celebrated strike at Shaista Khan's camp in Pune.

2.5 Battle of Umberkhind

Battle of Umberkhind took place on 3 February 1661 in the mountain range of Sahyadri near the city of Khopoli, Maharashtra,

India. The battle was fought between the Maratha army under Shivaji and General Kartalab Khan of the Mughal Empire. The Marathas defeated the Mughal forces. This battle was a great example of guerrilla warfare. On the orders of Aurangzeb, Shahista Khan sent Kartalab Khan and Rai Bagan to attack Rajgad Fort. Shivaji's men encountered them in a forest in the mountain hills, which was called the Umberkhind.2.5.1 Battle

After Aurangzeb's accession to the throne in 1659, he sent Shahista Khan as a viceroy of the Deccan with a large Mughal Army to enforce the treaty, which Mughals had signed with the Adilshahi of Bijapur. However, this territory was also fiercely contested by the Maratha ruler, Shivaji who had acquired a huge reputation after his killing of a Adilshahi general, Afzal Khan, in 1659. In January 1660, Shahista Khan arrived at Aurangabad and quickly advanced, seizing Pune area, the centre of Shivaji's realm. He also captured the fort of Chakan and Kalyan and north Konkan after heavy fighting with the Marathas. The Marathas were banned from entering into the city of Pune. Kartalab Khan and Rai Bagan were told to assist Shahista Khan in his campaign. Shahista Khan sent both Kartalab Khan and Rai Bagan to capture Rajgad Fort. So they went on their way with 20,000 soldiers for each of them. Shivaji wanted Kartalab Khan and the famous *Rai Bagan (Royal Tigress),* the wife of Deshmukh of Mahur Sarkar of Berar Subah *Raje Udaram,* to enter Umberkhind, so that they become easy prey to his preplanned guerilla technique. When the Mughals entered Umberkhind, a 15 miles passage, Shivaji's men started blowing horns. The whole Mughal army got stunned. Then the Marathas started attacking the Mughal Army with a barrage of arrows. Kartalab Khan and Rai Bagan along with the other Mughal soldiers tried to retaliate in emergency, but the forest was so dense and the Maratha Army was so quick and prepared, that the Mughals could not even see the enemy. The situation was such that Mughal soldiers were being killed by arrows and swords, without even, seeing where the enemy was, from where the blow is coming and without knowing where to shoot. A large number of the Mughal soldiers died in this way.

Rai Bagan then advised Kartalab Khan, that he should surrender himself to Shivaji and should ask for mercy. She said, "Shivaji is a lion and you have made a huge mistake by putting the whole army into the lion's jaw. You should not have chosen this path to attack Shivaji. Now, to save these dying soldiers, you should surrender yourself to Shivaji. Unlike Mughals, Shivaji shows amnesty for those who surrender." The battle lasted for an hour or two. And then Kartalab Khan on advise of *Rai Bagan*, sent the soldiers with a white flag for truce. They shouted "truce, truce!" and within a minute got encircled by Shivaji's men. Then on the condition of paying a large ransom and surrendering all their arms and clothes, Kartalab Khan was allowed to go back to his main Mughal camp. Shivaji then stationed his renowned general Netaji Palkar in Umberkhind to keep a check on the Mughals, if they come back.

2.6 Battle of Surat

Battle of Surat, also known as the Sack of Surat, was a land battle that took place on January 5, 1664, near the city of Surat, Gujarat, India between Maratha ruler Shivaji and Inayat Khan, a Mughal captain. The Marathas defeated the Mughal force, and sacked the city of Surat for six days.

According to James Grant Duff, a captain in the British India Regiment, Surat was attacked by Shivaji on 5 January 1664. Surat was a wealthy port city in the Mughal Empire and was useful for the Mughals as it was used for the sea trade of the Arabian Sea. The city was well populated mostly by Hindus and a few Muslims, especially the officials in the Mughal administration of the city. The attack was so sudden that the population had no chance to flee. The plunder was continued for six days and two-thirds of the city was burnt down. The loot was then transferred to Rajgad fort.

2.6.1 Background

As Shaista Khan, the Mughal governor, was in Deccan for more than three years fighting the Marathas, the financial condition of the Maratha Kingdom was dire. So to improve his finances, Shivaji planned to attack Surat, a key Mughal power centre, and a wealthy port town that generated a million rupees in taxes. His aim was to capture and loot the wealthy port city and bring all the loot to his main residence, the Raigad Fort.

2.6.2 Battle

2.6.2.1 Composition of Forces

Local Subedar, Inayat Khan who was appointed by Aurangzeb, had only 1000 men at his command. After attacking and then sacking the Mughal garrison, Shivaji attacked the Port of Surat and set the local shipping industry ablaze.

Shivaji was assisted by commanders along with cavalry of 10000.

2.6.2.2 Movement and clash of forces

Shivaji attacked Surat after demand for the tribute was rejected. The Mughal Sardar was very surprised by the suddenness of the attack, unwilling to face the Maratha forces, he hid himself in the Fort of Surat.

Surat was under attack for nearly three days, in which the Maratha Army looted all possible wealth from Mughal and Portuguese trading centers. The Maratha soldiers took away cash, gold, silver, pearls, rubies, diamonds and emeralds from the houses of rich merchants such as Virji Vora, Haji Zahid Beg, Haji Kasim and others. The business of Mohandas Parekh, the deceased broker of the Dutch East India Company, was spared as he was reputed as a charitable man. Similarly, Chhatrapati Shivaji did not plunder the houses of the foreign missionaries. The French traveller Francois Bernier wrote in his Travels in Mughal India.

I forgot to mention that during pillage of Sourate, Seva-ji, the Holy Seva-ji! Respected the habitation of the reverend father Ambrose, the *Capuchin* missionary. 'The Frankish Padres are good men', he said 'and shall not be attacked.'

Shivaji had to complete the sacking of Surat before the Mughal Empire at Delhi was alerted and he could not afford to spend much time attacking the British. Thus, Sir George Oxenden was able to successfully defend the British factory, a fortified warehouse-counting house-hostel.

2.6.3 Casualties

One Englishman named Anthony Smith, was captured by the Marathas, and funds were demanded from him. Smith wrote an account of him witnessing Shivaji ordering the cutting off of the heads and hands of those who concealed their wealth.[1] However, when Shivaji came to know and understand that Smith was poor, he freed him. When the Mughal Army finally approached on the fourth fateful day, Shivaji and his Maratha soldiers had already started their return southwards into the Deccan.

2.6.4 Aftermath

All this loot was successfully transported to the Deccan before the Mughal Empire at Delhi could get the news of the sacking of Surat. This wealth later was used for developing & strengthening the Maratha State. This event enraged the Mughal Emperor, Aurangzeb. The revenue of the Mughal Empire was reduced as trade did not flourish as much after Shivaji's raid on the Port of Surat. To take his revenge, the Mughal Emperor sent a veteran Rajput general, Jai Singh, to curb Shivaji's activities.

2.7 Battle of Purandar

The Battle of Purandar was fought between the Mughal Empire and Maratha Empire in 1665. The Mughal Emperor, Aurangzeb, appointed Jai Singh to lead a 14,000 strong army against Shivaji and deputed several Mughal commanders like Dilir Khan, Rai Singh, Sujan Singh and Daud Khan to serve Jai Singh in his campaign. to besiege Shivaji's fortress at Purandar.

After Mughal forces killed Maratha General, Murarbaji on 2 June 1665, Shivaji surrendered and gave up 23 of his fortresses.

2.7.1 Background

Shivaji Maharaj attacked six Mughal generals at Lal Mahal of Poona (Now Pune). Then Shivaji Maharaj sacked Surat, a prosperous port city back then which inhabited lots of rich merchants from all parts of India, China, Turkey, England and the Netherlands. Shivaji Maharaj got huge amount of wealth in this loot. Later, in 1665 Aurangzeb sent his general Mirza Raja Jai Singh to subdue Shivaji Maharaj and the Adil Shahi dynasty.

2.7.2 Siege of Purandar

Jai Singh besieged Purandar fort in 1665. He won the neighbouring Vajragad fort in the middle of April. He surrounded Purandar and attacked the walls of the fort with cannons. Marathas fought bravely. The commandant Murarbaji fought courageously. He with his selected 700 fighters made a sortie on Diler Khan, who was only second in command after Mirza Rajah Jai Singh. Diler Khan with his 5000 Afghans and some more troop of other races was trying to climb the hill. Marathas marched forward and attacked these Mughal enemy from all sides and fought severe fighting at close quarters. Murar Baji and his Maratha men slew 500 Pathan and Bahlia infantrymen. Murar Baji rushed towards Diler Khan. The later offered him high post under him and promised his life. Murar indignantly refused and was going to strike Diler Khan when the latter shot him down with an arrow. The garrison continued the struggle. But due to the firing of cannons 5 towers and one stockade won by enemies. The garrison had only 2000 Maratha soldiers against at least ten times that number of enemies. They had suffered heavy number of casualties in the 2 months' incessant fight. Shivaji found it futile to prolong and resist. The families of Maratha officers were sheltered inside the fort, so its capture would cause captivity. Due to this, Shivaji decided to meet Jai Singh and offer terms of peace. If these were rejected, he would make alliance with Adil Shah by restoring Konkan and continuing war against the Mughals with renewed vigour.

Following their victory in the Battle of Purandar, the Mughals attempted to take Sanganer Fort from the Marathas, but they refused. As a result, Diler Himmat Khan stormed Sanganer Fort, took it, and massacred 30,000 Marathas there.

2.7.3 Treaty of Purandar

Shivaji On the way to meet Jai Singh I.

The Treaty of Purandar was signed on 11 June 1665, between Jai Singh I, commander of the Mughal Empire, and Shivaji. Shivaji Maharaj was forced to sign the agreement after

Jai Singh besieged Purandar fort. When Shivaji Maharaj realised that war with the Mughal Empire would only cause damage to his empire with possibility of his men suffering heavy losses, he chose to enter the treaty instead of leaving his men under the Mughals.

2.7.3.1 Terms

Following are the main points of the treaty:

- Shivaji kept twelve forts, along with an area worth an income of 100,000 (1 lakh) huns.

- Shivaji was required to help the Mughals whenever and wherever required.

- Shivaji's son Sambhaji was tasked with the command of a 5,000-strong force to fight for Mughals as Mansabdar.

- If Shivaji wanted to claim the Konkan area under Bijapur's control, he would have to pay 4 million (40 lakh) hons to the Mughals.

- He had to give up his 23 forts, which include Purandar, Rudramal, Kondana, Karnala, Lohagad, Isagad, Tung, Tikona, Rohida fort, Nardurga, Mahuli, Bhandardurga, Palaskhol, Rupgad, Bakhtgad, Morabkhan, Manikgad (Raigad), Saroopgad, Sagargad, Marakgad, Ankola, Songad, and Mangad.

Along with these requirements, Shivaji agreed to visit Agra to meet Aurangzeb for further political talks.

2.7.4 Aftermath

Jai Singh stopped his attack on Purandar, allowing 7000 residents of the fort to come out which included 4000 Maratha warriors. Shivaji handed over his forts to Jai Singh. Later Shivaji and his forces fought along with Jai Singh against Adil Shah of Bijapur but failed to win.Later Shivaji travelled to Agra to Aurangzeb's court. But Aurangzeb put him under house arrest for a few months. Shivaji managed to escape and returned home. Aurangzeb blamed Jai Singh's son Ram Singh for Shivaji's escape and demoted him.

2.8 Battle of Sinhagad

Sinhagad fort

The Battle of Sinhagad took place during the night of 4 February 1670 on the fort of Sinhagad (then known as Kondhana after the sage Kaundinya), near the city of Pune, Maharashtra, India.

2.8.1 Background

A 20th century depiction of Tanaji Malusare's famous vow during Kondana campaign by painter M.V. Dhurandhar

The battle was fought between Koli Subedar Tanaji Malusare, commander of the Marathas under Shivaji and Udaybhan Singh Rathore, a Rajput fortkeeper under Jai Singh I who worked for the Mughal emperor Aurangzeb.

2.8.2 Battle

Sinhagad was one of the first forts which Chhatrapati Shivaji Maharaj re-captured from the Mughals. The capture was made possible by scaling the walls at night with ladders made of rope. In this battle both Udaybhan Rathore and Tanhaji both were killed, but the fort was captured by the Marathas. The battle and Tanhaji's exploits are still a popular subject for Marathi ballad.

2.8.3 Siege of fort

Tanaji Malusare and 300 hand-picked Mavle infantry, assisted by some Koli guides, scaled the hillside using rope ladders. They advanced into the fort, killing the sentinels. The alarm was sounded and the Mughals took some time to arm themselves and come out, allowing the Marathas to secure their footing.

During the attack, Malusare scaled a steep cliff that led to the fort with the assistance of a monitor lizard called Yashwanti (also referred to as ghorpad in Marathi language). This type of lizard had been tamed since the 15th century, and Yashwanti was trained to pull the rope up the cliffs for Malusare and wind it around the fort's bastion.

Climbing up the fort, the Marathas were intercepted by the garrison and combat ensued between the guards and several infiltrators that had managed to climb up. Tanaji and his Mavala infantrymen climbed the Kalyan darwaza (transl. Gate), one of the two main gates of the fort. The garrison fought desperately, but the Maratha Mavales wreaked havoc in their ranks. Tanaji and Udaybhan fought each other intensely, killing each other after a one on one combat. Tanaji's shield broke during the battle.

The Maratha soldiers then set fire to the cavalry's huts, and the blaze informed Shivaji at Raigad that Kondhana has been captured.

2.8.4 Aftermath

It is said that when Shivaji got the information about the victory and the loss of Tanaji's life during the battle, he exclaimed "Gad aala pan sinh gela" (Devnagari: गड आला पण सिंह गेला) (transl. "The fort has been captured but we lost the lion"). A bust of Tanaji Malusare was established on the fort in the memory of his contribution and sacrifice. The fort was also renamed Sinhagad to honor his memory.

2.9 Battle of Salher

The Battle of Salher was a battle fought between the Marathas and the Mughal Empire in February 1672 CE. The battle was fought near the fort of Salher in the Nashik district. The result was a decisive victory for the Marathas. This battle is considered particularly significant as it is the first pitched battle in which the Mughal Empire lost to the Marathas.

2.9.1 Background

The Treaty of Purandar (1665) required Shivaji to cede 23 forts to the Mughals. Strategically important forts, which were fortified with garrisons, such as Sinhagad, Purandar, Lohagad, Karnala, and Mahuli were turned over to the Mughal empire. At the time of this treaty, the Nashik region, that contained the forts Salher and Mulher, was firmly in the Mughal Empire's hands since 1636. The signing of this treaty resulted in Shivaji's visit to Agra and after his famous escape from the same in September 1666, 2 years of 'uneasy truce' followed.

The period between 1670-1672 saw a dramatic rise in Shivaji's power and territory. Shivaji's armies successfully conducted raids at Baglan, Khandesh, and Surat and retook more than a dozen forts. This culminated with a decisive victory against a Mughal army of more than 40,000 on an open field near Salher.

2.9.2 The Battle

Senapati Prataprao Gujar and along with his army of 15,000 captured the Mughal forts Aundha, Patta, Trimbak and attacked Salher and Mulher in January 1671. This led Aurangzeb to send two of his generals Ikhlas Khan and Bahlol Khan along with 12,000 horsemen to reclaim Salher. In October 1671, the Mughal Army laid siege on Salher. In return Shivaji commanded his two commanders Peshwa Moropant Pingle and Sardar Prataprao Gujar reclaim the fort.

50,000 Mughals had besieged the fort for more than 6 months. Shivaji knew the strategic importance of Salher as it was the main fort on important trade routes. Dilerkhan had also attacked Pune in the meanwhile and Shivaji could not save Pune because his main armies were away. Shivaji devised a plan to divert Dilerkhan by forcing him reach Salher. He ordered Moropant who was in South Konkan and Prataprao who was raiding near

Aurangabad to meet and attack Mughals at Salher to relieve the fort. In his letter to his commanders Shivaji had written 'Go to the north and attack Salher and defeat the enemy'. Both the Maratha forces met near the village of Vani, they bypassed the Mughal camp at Nashik and reached near Salher. The total Maratha strength was of 40,000(20,000 infantry + 20,000 cavalry). The terrain was not suitable for cavalry battle hence the Maratha commanders decided to lure, split and finish the Mughal forces at different places. As per the plan Prataprao Gujar stormed the Mughals with 5,000 cavalry and killed many unprepared soldiers. After half an hour the Mughals became fully ready and Prataprao started to flee with his army. The entire Mughal cavalry of 25,000 started chasing the Marathas. Prataprao lured mughal cavalry in a pass 25 km away from Salher where the 15,000 cavalry under Anandrao Makaji was hiding. Prataprao turned his back in the pass and attacked the Mughals once again. The 15,000 fresh cavalry under Anandrao blocked the other end of the pass and Mughals were surrounded from all sides. The fresh Maratha cavalry soundly defeated the tired Mughal cavalry in 2-3 hours. Thousands of Mughals fled the Battle.

Moropant later surrounded and attacked the 25,000 strong Mughal infantry at Salher with his 20,000 infantry. Prominent maratha sardar and Shivaji's childhood friend Suryaji Kakde was killed by a Zamburak cannon in the battle.

The battle lasted for an entire day and it is estimated that around 10,000 men were killed on both the sides. The Mughal military machines (consisting of cavalry, infantry, and artillery) were outmatched by the light cavalry of the Marathas. The imperial Mughal armies were completely routed and the Marathas gave them a crushing defeat. 6,000 horses, an equal number of camels, 125 elephants, and an entire Mughal train were captured by the victorious Maratha Army. Other than this, a large amount of goods, treasures, gold, jewels, clothes, and carpets were seized by the Marathas.

The Sabhasad Bakhar describes the battle as follows "As the fighting began, such a (cloud of) dust arose that for a space of a three-kilometer square, friend and foe could not be distinguished. Elephants were killed. Ten thousand men on the two sides became corpses. The horses, camels, elephants (killed) were beyond counting. A flood of blood streamed (in the battlefield). The blood formed a muddy pool and in it (people) began to sink, so (deep) was the mud."

2.9.3 Outcome

The battle resulted in a decisive Maratha victory which resulted in the liberation of Salher. Further, the nearby fort of Mulher was also taken from the Mughals as a consequence of this battle. 22 *wazirs* of note were taken as prisoners and Ikhlas Khan and Bahlol Khan were captured. Among the Mughal soldiers who were prisoners around one or two thousand escaped. The notable *Panchazari* Sardar of the Maratha army Suryajirao Kakade was killed in this battle and was revered for his ferocity during the battle. Approximately a dozen Maratha *sardars* were gifted for their remarkable achievements in the battle and the two officers (Sardar Moropant Pingle and Sardar Prataprao Gujar) were specially rewarded.

2.9.4 Consequences

Most of Shivaji's victories until this battle had been through means of guerilla warfare, but the Maratha's use of light cavalry on the Salher battlefield against the apparently superior Mughal forces proved effective. This grand victory resulted in the saint Ramdas to write his famous letter to Shivaji in which he addresses him as Gajpati (Lord of Elephants), Haypati (Lord of Cavalry), Gadpati (Lord of Forts), and Jalpati (Master of the High Seas). Although not as a direct outcome of this battle, a couple of years later in 1674 Shivaji Maharaj was crowned as an Emperor (or *Chhatrapati*) of his realm.

2.10 Maratha occupation of Kolistan (1672)

Maratha occupation of Kolistan (lit. 'Land of the Koli people') in the year 1672 was a campaign in which the Maratha army under Shivaji and his son Sambhaji and Peshwa Moropant defeated the allied forces of Koli kings of Jawhar and Ramnagar Mughal Empire and the British Troops. The Marathas captured the region called Kolistan encompassing the Jawhar, Mokhada, Wada, Talasari, Vikramgad talukas in present day Palghar district of Maharashtra and the regions Southern Gujarat controlled by the Koli king of Ramnagar.

2.10.1 Background

Shivaji had sacked the city of Surat in the year 1664. He passed through the territories of Koli Kings of Jawhar and Ramnagar and they had helped him. The Treaty of Purandar was signed between Marathas and the Mughals in the year 1665. After the treaty the Koli Kings became vassals of the Mughal Empire. When Shivaji sacked Surat for a second time in the year 1670, the Koli Kings did not help him. Hence Shivaji wanted to capture the crucial territories of Kolistan which lied just to the South of Surat.

While the first and second sack of surat Shivaji harmed and looted the British officers and their camps.

Thus, the british officers wanted to avenge Shivaji, they helped Koli kings of Jawahar and koli kings of Ramnagar. Capturing Kolistan would have given Shivaji an access to the Mughal province of Gujarat. Shivaji, his son Sambhaji and Peshwa Moropant Pingle arrived to capture Kolistan from the Koli Kings and Mughal empire. Allied forces of Koli state of Jawhar,Koli state of Ramnagar and the british officers with Mughal General Dilir Khan confronted Marathas in kolistan region. This was the first crucial military campaign in the life of Sambhaji.

2.10.2 Campaign of the Marathas

Shivaji, Sambhaji and Moropant left the capital with a force of 7,000 men. The Marathas controlled regions as far as Mahuli fort in Thane district hence they attacked Kolistan from the south. Sambhaji led the Maratha forces and attacked Koli king Vikramshah's capital city of Jawhar. Vikramshah and the british officers which helped him fled the city without fighting. They fled to senior Mughal Sardar Dilir Khan who was stationed at Nashik with a large army. Rest of the soldiers in Vikramshah's army were assimilated into the Maratha army. The Marathas then attacked the Koli state of Ramnagar in southern Gujarat and captured the city. The Koli king of Ramnagar Som Shah also fled without offering any resistance to invading Maratha army. Marathas had stretched their territories up to 10 miles south of Surat which was highly unaffordable for the Mughals. Hence Diler Khan decided to help the Koli Kings and the british officers to capture the region once again.

2.11 Battle of Vikramgad

Shivaji was resting at jawhar, and his son Sambhaji with Peshwa Moropant Pingle stayed at Vikramgad. Diler Khan immediately with his General Khizr Khan with an army about 10,000 immediately arrived to capture Kolistan back from the Marathas.Dilir Khan and Khizr Khan decided to attack the Marathas led by Sambhaji in a full fledged battle. The two forces clashed near the town of Vikramgad.The battle began with initial skirmishes which were inconclusive. Both the forces clashed with other and a fierce battle went on 2-3 hours. Both sides had heavy casualties but battle was still inconclusive till afternoon. Then the Marathas started to gain an upper hand in the battle, inflicting very heavy casualties on the Mughal army. Khizr Khan was himself wounded in the severe battle. Seeing this the Mughal army started to flee towards Nashik. The Marathas routed the fleeing Mughal army. Victory in the battle of Vikramgad further consolidated the Maratha hold on Kolistan.

2.11.1 Aftermath

The Maratha occupation of Kolistan gave them access to the province of Gujarat. The Marathas extended their border to ten miles south of Surat, threatening the Mughal trading center of Surat. Shivaji then constructed two new forts namely Parner and Pindwol in Kolistan to strengthen his control over the region.

2.11.2 Legacy

This was the first campaign led by a 15-year-old prince Sambhaji. His success in his first campaign as a military leader enhanced his reputation among the other regional powers.

2.12 Battle of Bhupalgarh

The Battle of Bhupalgarh occurred between the Mughal Empire and Maratha Empire in 1679. After a fierce bloody resistance to the siege lasting over 55 days, the battle resulted in the razing of the fort of Bhupalgarh and a decisive victory for the Mughals over the Maratha Shivaji, under general Diler Khan.

After terrible fighting, the Mughals captured the fortress and its stores and enslaved the garrison. Diler Khan then defeated Maratha reinforcements nearby and razed the fort to the ground.

2.12.1 Result

The Maratha king Shivaji was defeated by the Mughals in this battle. Also the fort of Bhupalgarh was razed by the Mughals.

2.13 Battle of Sangamner

The Battle of Sangamner was fought between the Mughal Empire and Maratha Empire in 1679. This was the last battle in which the Maratha King Shivaji fought. The Mughals had ambushed Shivaji with a large force when he was returning from the sack of Jalna. The Marathas engaged in battle with the Mughals for three days but lost to the Mughals.

Shivaji successfully escaped with 500 soldiers while the combat continued until Maratha general, Sidhoji Nimbalkar was killed along with 2000 soldiers whereas Santaji Ghorpade finally took to flight after being routed, with Hambir Rao injured and many Maratha soldiers arrested. Shivaji returned to Raigad safely early in december that year.

2.14 Battle of Dindori

A fierce obstinate battle was fought for hours between the two sides between Vani and Dindori. Daud Khan, Ikhilas Khan, Sangram Khan and other important Mughal nobles fought with great courage using their artillery, though with limited advantage. On the Maratha side, Shivaji himself was conducting the operations in this one of the few open battles fought man to man. The battle ended with about 3000 Mughal troops dead and a number of Mughal officers captured. The Marathas also captured about 4000 horses. The Mughal governor of Dindori, Sangram Khan, was allowed to join Shivaji's service. In this way Shivaji won a great victory in this battle which neutralized Mughal power in this region for quite some time.

CHAPTER 3

Battles after the death of Shivaji

3.1 War of 27 Years

War of 27 years was a series of battles fought between Marathas and Mughals from 1681 to 1707 in the Indian subcontinent. It was a series of battles. The war started in 1680 with the Mughal emperor Aurangzeb's invasion of the Maratha enclave in Bijapur established by Shivaji. The war can be broken down into three distinct phases :

- Marathas under Sambhaji (1681–1689).

- Marathas under Rajaram (1689–1700).

- Marathas under Maharani Tarabai (1700–1707).

It was a long snakes and ladders war game involving a quarter of a century and innumerable long and short battles. The war ended after the death of Aurangzeb in 1707, because of unstable later Mughals. It also paved the way for the Maratha expansion in the North.

3.2 Mughal–Maratha Wars

The Mughal–Maratha Wars, sometimes referred to as a whole as the Deccan War or the Maratha War of Independence, were a set of wars fought between the Maratha Empire and the Mughal Empire from 1680 to 1707.

This war begun in 1680 by the Mughal Emperor Aurangzeb's invasion of the Maratha Enclave in Bijapur, which was established by the Maratha leader Shivaji. After the death of Aurangzeb, Marathas defeated the Mughals in Delhi and Bhopal, and extended their empire up to Peshawar by 1758.

3.2.1 Marathas under Sambhaji (1681–1689)

Sambhaji led the Marathas for the first nine years of the Deccan Wars.

In the first half of 1681, many Mughal contingents were dispatched to lay siege to Maratha forts in present-day Gujarat, Maharashtra, Karnataka, and Madhya Pradesh. Sambhaji provided shelter to the emperor's rebel son Sultan Muhammad Akbar, which angered Aurangzeb. In September 1681, after settling his dispute with the royal house of Mewar, Aurangzeb began his journey to Deccan to conquer the relatively young Maratha Empire. He arrived at Aurangabad, the Mughal headquarters in the Deccan and made it his capital. Mughal contingents in the region numbered about 500,000. It was a disproportionate war in all senses. By the end of 1681, the Mughal forces had laid siege to Fort Ramsej. But the Marathas did not succumb to this onslaught. The attack was well received and it took the Mughals seven years to take the fort. In December 1681, Sambhaji attacked Janjira, but his first attempt failed. At the same time one of the Aurangzeb's generals, Husain Ali Khan, attacked Northern Konkan. Sambhaji left Janjira and attacked Husain Ali Khan and pushed him back to Ahmednagar. Aurangzeb tried to sign a deal with the Portuguese to allow trade ships to harbour in Goa. This would have allowed him to open another supply route to Deccan via the sea. This news reached Sambhaji. He attacked the Portuguese territories and forced them back to the Goan coast. But the viceroy of Alvor was able to defend the Portuguese headquarters. By this time the huge Mughal army had started gathering on the borders of Deccan. It was clear that southern India was headed for a large, sustained conflict.

In late 1683, Aurangzeb moved to Ahmednagar. He divided his forces in two and put his two princes, Shah Alam and Azam Shah, in charge of each division. Shah Alam was to attack South Konkan via the Karnataka border while Azam Shah would attack

Khandesh and northern Maratha territory. Using a pincer strategy, these two divisions planned to encircle Marathas from the south and north to isolate them. The beginning went quite well. Shah Alam crossed the Krishna river and entered Belgaum. From there he entered Goa and started marching north via Konkan. As he pushed further, he was continuously harassed by Marathas forces. They ransacked his supply chains and reduced his forces to starvation. Finally Aurangzeb sent Ruhulla Khan to his rescue and brought him back to Ahmednagar. The first pincer attempt failed.

After the 1684 monsoon, Aurangzeb's other general Shahbuddin Khan directly attacked the Maratha capital, Raigad. Maratha commanders successfully defended Raigad. Aurangzeb sent Khan Jehan to help, but Hambirao Mohite, commander-in-chief of the Maratha army, defeated him in a fierce battle at Patadi. The second division of the Maratha army attacked Shahbuddin Khan at Pachad, inflicting heavy losses on the Mughal army.

In early 1685, Shah Alam attacked south again via the Gokak-Dharwar route, but Sambhaji's forces harassed him continuously on the way and finally he had to give up and thus failed to close the loop a second time. In April 1685, Aurangzeb changed his strategy. He planned to consolidate his power in the south by undertaking expeditions to the Muslim kingdoms of Golkonda and Bijapur. Both of them were allies of Marathas and Aurangzeb was not fond of them. He broke his treaties with both kingdoms, attacked them and captured them by September 1686. Taking this opportunity, Marathas launched an offensive on the North coast and attacked Bharuch. They were able to evade the Mughal army sent their way and came back with minimum damage. Marathas tried to win Mysore through diplomacy. Sardar Kesopant Pingle was running negotiations, but the fall of Bijapur to the Mughals turned the tides and Mysore was reluctant to join Marathas. Sambhaji successfully courted several Bijapur sardars to join the Maratha army.

Sambhaji led the fight but was captured by the Mughals and killed. His wife and son (Shivaji's grandson) were held captive by Aurangzeb for twenty years.

3.2.2 Execution of Sambhaji

Stone arch at Tulapur confluence where Sambhaji was executed.

After the fall of Bijapur and Golkonda, Aurangzeb turned his attention again to the Marathas but his first few attempts had little impact. In January 1688, Sambhaji called together his commanders for a strategic meeting at Sangameshwar in Konkan to decide on the final blow to oust Aurangzeb from the Deccan. To execute the decision of the meeting quickly, Sambhaji sent ahead most of his comrades and stayed back with a few of his trustworthy men, including Kavi Kalash.

Ganoji Shirke, one of Sambhaji's brothers-in-law, turned traitor and helped Aurangzeb's commander Muqarrab Khan to locate, reach and attack Sangameshwar while Sambhaji was still there. The relatively small Maratha force fought back although they were surrounded from all sides. Sambhaji was captured on 1 February 1689 and a subsequent rescue attempt by the Marathas was repelled on 11 March. He refused to bow down to Aurangzeb, so he was beheaded.

3.3 Marathas under King Rajaram (1689 to 1700)

To Aurangzeb, the Marathas seemed all but dead by end of 1689. But this would prove to be almost a fatal blunder. The death of Sambhaji had rekindled the spirit of the Maratha forces, which made Aurangzeb's mission impossible. Sambhaji's younger brother Rajaram was now given the title of Chhatrapati (Emperor). In March 1690, the Maratha commanders, under the leadership of Santaji Ghorpade launched the single most daring attack on Mughal army. They not only attacked the army, but sacked the tent where the Aurangzeb himself slept. Luckily Aurangzeb was elsewhere but his private force and many of his bodyguards were killed. However, this was followed by a betrayal in the Maratha camp. Raigad fell to the treachery of Suryaji Pisal. Sambhaji's queen, Yesubai and their son, Shahu I, were captured.

Mughal forces, led by Zulfikar Khan, continued this offensive further south. They attacked fort Panhala. The Maratha killedar of Panhala defended the fort and inflicted heavy losses on

Mughal army. Finally Aurangzeb himself had to come and Panhala was surrendered.

3.3.1 Maratha capital moved to Jinji

Maratha ministers realised that the Mughals would move on Vishalgad. They insisted that Rajaram leave Vishalgad for Senji (Gingee) (in present Tamil Nadu), which had been captured by Shivaji during his southern conquests and was now to be the new Maratha capital. Rajaram travelled south under escort of Khando Ballal and his men.

Aurangzeb was frustrated with Rajaram's successful escape. Keeping most of his force in Maharashtra, he sent a small number to keep Rajaram in check. This small force was destroyed by an attack from two Maratha generals, Santaji Ghorpade and Dhanaji Jadhav, who then they joined Ramchandra Bavadekar in Deccan. Bavdekar, Vithoji Chavan and Raghuji Bhosale had reorganised most of the Maratha army after defeats at Panhala and Vishalgad.

In late 1691, Bavdekar, Pralhad Niraji, Santaji, Dhanaji and several Maratha sardars met in the Maval region and reformed the strategy. Aurangzeb had taken four major forts in Sahyadrais and was sending Zulfikar khan to subdue the fort Ginjee. So according to new Maratha plan, Santaji and Dhanaji would launch offensives in the East to keep rest of the Mughal forces scattered. Others would focus in Maharashtra and would attack a series of forts around southern Maharashtra and northern Karnataka to divide Mughal won territories in two, thereby posing significant challenge to enemy supply chains. Having a strong navy established by Shivaji, the Marathas could now extend this divide into the sea, checking any supply routes from Surat to south.

Now war was fought from the Malwa plateau to the east coast. Such was the strategy of Maratha commanders to counter the might of the Mughals. Maratha generals Ramchandrapant Amatya and Shankaraji Niraji maintained the Maratha stronghold in the rugged terrains of Sahyadri.

Through cavalry movements, Santaji Ghorpade and Dhanaji Jadhav defeated the Mughals. In the Battle of Athani, Santaji defeated Kasim Khan, a noted Mughal general.

3.3.2 Fall of Jinji (Jan 1698)

Aurangzeb by now had realised that the war he had started was much more serious than he had originally thought. He decided to regroup his forces and rethink his strategy. He sent an ultimatum to Zulfikar Khan to capture Jinji or be stripped of the titles. Zulfikar Khan tightened the Siege, but Rajaram escaped and was safely escorted to Deccan by Dhanaji Jadhav and the Shirke brothers. Haraji Mahadik's son took command of Jinji and bravely defended the city against Julfikar Khan and Daud Khan until its fall in January 1698. This gave Rajaram ample amount of time to reach Vishalgad.

After significant Mughal losses, Jinji was captured in a classic Pyrrhic victory. The fort had done its work: for seven years the three hills of Jinji had kept a large contingent of Mughal forces occupied while inflicting heavy losses. It had significantly depleted Mughal resources in the region, from the treasury to material.

Marathas would soon witness an unpleasant development of their own making. Dhanaji Jadhav and Santaji Ghorpade had a simmering rivalry, which was kept in check by the councilman Pralhad Niraji. But after Niraji's death, Dhanaji grew bold and attacked Santaji. Nagoji Mane, one of Dhanaji's men, killed Santaji. The news of Santaji's death greatly encouraged Aurangzeb and the Mughal army.

But by this time the Mughals were no longer the army they were earlier feared to be. Aurangzeb, against the advice of several of his experienced generals, continued the war.

3.3.3 Revival of Maratha fortunes

The Marathas again consolidated and began a counter-offensive. Rajaram appointed Dhanaji Jadhav as commander-in-chief and the army was split into three divisions, headed by Jadhav himself, Parshuram Timbak and Shankar Narayan. Jadhav defeated a large Mughal force near Pandharpur and Narayan defeated Sarja Khan in Pune. Khanderao Dabhade, who led a division under Jadhav, took Baglan and Nashik, while Nemaji Shinde, a commander with Narayan, scored a major victory at Nandurbar.

Enraged at these defeats, Aurangzeb took charge and launched another counter-offensive. He laid siege to Panhala and attacked the fort of Satara. A seasoned Maratha commander, Prayagji Prabhu, defended Satara for a good six months but surrendered in April 1700, just before the onset of the monsoon. This foiled Aurangzeb's strategy to clear as many forts before the monsoon as possible.

3.4 Marathas under Tarabai

In March 1700, Rajaram died. His queen, Tarabai, who was daughter of the Maratha commander-in-chief Hambirrao Mohite, took charge of the Maratha army and continued fighting for the next seven years.

Aurangzeb leads the Mughal Army during the Battle of Satara

After the Battle of Satara, Aurangzeb contested for every inch of Deccan region at great cost of life and money. Aurangzeb drove west, deep into Maratha territory notably conquering Satara (the Maratha capital) the Marathas expanded eastwards into Mughal lands Hyderabad. Aurangzeb waged continuous war in the Deccan for more than two decades with no resolution and thus lost about a fifth of his army.

Signs of strain were showing in the Mughal camp in late 1701. Asad Khan, Julfikar Khan's father, counselled Aurangzeb to end the war and turn around. The expedition had already taken a giant toll, much larger than originally planned, on the empire and it looked possible that 175 years of Mughal rule might crumble due to being involved in a war that was not winnable.

By 1704, Aurangzeb conquered Torana, Rajgad and some other handful forts mostly by bribing maratha commanders, but he had spent four precious years for this. It was slowly dawning to him that after 24 years of constant war, he was not succeeded to annex the Maratha State.

The final Maratha counter-offensive gathered momentum in the North, where Mughal provinces fell one by one. They were not in position to defend because the royal treasuries had been sucked dry and no armies were available. In 1705, two Maratha army factions crossed Narmada. One, under the leadership of Nemaji Shinde, hit as far north as Bhopal; the second, headed by Khanderao Dabhade, struck Bharoch and the west. With his 8000 men, Dabhade attacked and defeated Mahomed Khan's forces numbering almost fourteen thousand.

This left entire Gujarat coast wide open for Marathas. They immediately tightened their grip on Mughal supply chains. By 1705 end, Marathas had penetrated Mughal possession of Central

India and Gujarat. Nemaji Shinde defeated Mughals on the Malwa plateau.

In 1706, Mughals started retreating from Maratha dominions. In Maharashtra, Aurangzeb became despondent. He started negotiations with the Marathas, then cut them abruptly and marched on the small kingdom of Wakinara whose Naik rulers traced their lineage to the royal family of the Vijaynagar empire.

His new opponents had never been fond of the Mughals and had sided with the Marathas. Jadhav marched into Sahyadris and won almost all the major forts back in a short time, while those of Satara and Parali were taken by Parshuram Timbak, and Narayan took Sinhgad. Jadhav then turned around, taking his forces to help the Naiks at Wakinara. Wakinara fell but the Naik royal family escaped.

3.4.1 Aurangzeb's death

Aurangzeb had now given up all hope and planned a retreat to Burhanpur. Jadhav attacked and defeated his rearguard but Aurangzeb was able to reach his destination with the help of Zulfikar Khan. He died of a fever on 21 February 1707.

3.5 Aftermath of the war

Marathas expanded their territory to include Malwa after the Battle of Delhi and Battle of Bhopal in 1737. And by 1757, the Maratha Empire had reached Delhi.

Maratha Empire became major power in the Indian sub-continent after 1720s. The above map is of 1760.

The Mughal empire was split in regional kingdoms, with the Nizam of Hyderabad, Nawab of Oudh and Nawab of Bengal quick to assert the nominal independence of their lands.

The Mughal–Maratha Wars had a significant impact on the political and social landscape of India. The wars weakened both the Mughal and Maratha empires, paving the way for European colonial powers to establish themselves in India. The wars also contributed to the decline of the Mughal Empire, which was already facing internal political and economic challenges. The Marathas, on the other hand, emerged as a major power in India, and their influence continued to grow in the following centuries.

CHAPTER 4

Battles under Sambhaji

Shivaji was succeeded by his son Sambhaji, after his death in April 1680. His son Sambhaji Raje was also a genius military commander like him. Sambhaji fought many victorious battles in his short life. Sambhaji managed to defend the Maratha Empire against the overwhelmingly strong Mughal Empire. Sambhaji fought many battles in his reign against his enemies such as Mughal Empire, Siddis of Janjira, Portuguese of Goa and North Konkan(Mumbai & Ghodbunder fort), Chikkadevaraya of Mysore.

4.1 Sacking of Burhanpur (1681)

The Sacking of Burhanpur (31 January 1681-2 February 1681) refers to the looting of the wealthy Mughal city Burhanpur in Madhya Pradesh by the Maratha ruler Sambhaji. The Maratha army commanded by Sambhaji and Hambirrao Mohite attacked and plundered the city for three days. The Marathas got a huge loot and returned to Raigad by evading Mughal forces.

4.1.1 Background

Sambhaji ascended to throne after the death of his father Shivaji in 1680. He was crowned on 16 January 1681 at the Raigad Fort. His coronation ceremony was attended by more than 50,000 people. A large amount of money was spent on the function, and Sambhaji wanted to replenish his depleted treasury.

The Mughal emperor Aurangzeb had finished his campaign in Rajputana and was preparing for a full-scale invasion of the Deccan Plateau. Sambhaji knew that the Maratha Empire was heading into a sustained conflict against the overwhelmingly larger Mughal Empire. He wanted to fill the Maratha treasury before the arrival of Aurangzeb in Deccan. Sambhaji also wanted to gain a psychological edge over his opponent Aurangzeb by scoring the first victory.

4.1.2 Maratha Plan

Sambhaji called a strategic meeting of his advisors and senior generals at Raigad, just after his coronation. Sambhaji and Maratha generals decided to attack and plunder Burhanpur as it was an important trading center and a very rich city. The distance between Raigad Fort and Burhanpur was more than 500 kilometres. The city was heavily fortified and guarded by a force of 8,000.

Sambhaji had got the news that Bahadurkhan Kokaltash, the Subedar of Burhanpur was going to Aurangabad for his nephew's wedding with a girl from the royal family of Abul Hasan Qutb Shah. Bahadurkhan took a force 3,000 with him for the wedding. Hence Burhanpur was left with an army of 5,000 under Bahadurkhan's deputy Kakar Khan. Sambhaji decided to further bifurcate the force at Burhanpur by feigning a move to attack Surat, forcing the Mughals at Burhanpur to send reinforcement to Surat, which had been sacked by Shivaji twice before.

4.1.3 Sacking of Burhanpur

Hambirrao Mohite reached the forests near Burhanpur with a 15,000 strong cavalry force. Kakar Khan gathered civilian forces and decided to attack Hambirrao at midnight. As he came out of the city gates, Sambhaji himself attacked from the old trenches with a cavalry force of 4,000. Sambhaji's force routed the ill-prepared Mughal garrison. Sambhaji then left 200-300 soldiers at the main city gate and left for Bahadurpura, the richest suburb of the city. Sambhaji started to loot the houses of the richest merchants which were shown to him by his spies. Hambirrao's force soon joined Sambhaji and the combined Maratha force started looting the city. Hambirrao then sealed the city's entrances to ensure that the word of the attack doesn't spread out. Marathas looted the city consecutively for three days. Marathas earned a loot estimated to be around 2 crore rupees. The Marathas also captured the city fort and arrested Kakar Khan.

Bahadurkhan got the news and immediately left Aurangabad with a large army to save Burhanpur. When Marathas heard this they immediately fled the city, as they were far away from Maratha territory.

4.1.4 Withdrawal of Maratha forces

Sambhaji left Burhanpur and started marching towards Raigad. Bahadurkhan left Aurangabad with a force of around

20,000 to seize the loot back from the Marathas. Sambhaji divided his forces into three divisions.

There were two routes to reach Raigad, a shorter one via Dharangao-Chopda and a longer one via Erandol. Bahadurkhan was waiting for Sambhaji's forces at the first route. Sambhaji's first division under Mulla Kazi Haider disguised as envoys took this route. Bahadurkhan arrested them all but they convinced him that Sambhaji would choose the longer route to avoid his forces. After some time the second division of Maratha force consisting of 3,000 soldiers passed via the same route without any loot. Bahadurkhan did not attack them as he was concerned with securing the loot. Bahadurkhan was convinced after seeing this force that Sambhaji has opted for the longer route and left for Erandol. Three hours after Bahadurkhan had left the first route, the entire remaining Maratha army (Third division) took the loot via the same Dharangaon-Chopda route towards the Maratha stronghold of Salher. And the Marathas reached Raigad shortly thereafter.

Meanwhile, Bahadurkhan had left Aurangabad hastily with a large army leaving only few soldiers in Aurangabad. Seeing this opportunity a Maratha sardar named Suryaji Jakhde attacked Aurangabad with a force of 7,000 via Paithan. Bahadurkhan immediately rushed to Aurangabad via Fardapur and Suryaji Jakhde had to retreat from the city.

4.1.5 Assassination attempt on Sambhaji

Aurangzeb had stationed a few of his elite horsemen called Ahadi, in every important Mughal city. Their job was to locate and kill the leader of enemy forces in case of an attack. When Sambhaji left Burhanpur for Raigad, five Ahadi horsemen from Burhanpur started to chase the returning Maratha army. Sambhaji went to Vani with a small force to visit Saptashringi temple, and was attacked, but he managed to kill the 5 assassins in the fight.

4.2 Siege of Janjira (1682)

The siege of Janjira (1682) was a military conflict and a part of the Mughal-Maratha wars. It was fought between the Maratha Empire led by Sambhaji and Siddis of Janjira, allies of the Mughal Empire. Maratha emperor Sambhaji personally besieged the fort of Murud-Janjira in 1682 to stop Siddi's intrusions into Maratha territories and to capture the strategically important fort of Janjira.

4.2.1 Background

Mughal emperor Aurangzeb had arrived in the Deccan to conquer the Deccan Plateau in 1681. His first goal was to conquer the newly established Maratha Empire in Maharashtra. Aurangzeb wanted to encircle the Maratha Empire from all sides. He ordered his allies and enemies of Maratha Empire such as Siddis of Janjira, Wodeyars of Mysore and Portuguese of Goa to attack the Maratha Empire. In addition Sambhaji knew the strategic importance of Janjira, he had an ambition to capture it. Hence, Sambhaji decided to capture Janjira personally.

4.2.2 Plan of Marathas

Sambhaji had planned to Janjira by ruse, he had sent a party in 1681 under the leadership of senior Maratha General Kondaji Farzand under the pretext of a fake fight with Sambhaji. Kondaji and his men told Siddi about their fight with Sambhaji and asked for a post in his army. Siddi Khairiyat was happy at the defection of Kondaji at his side. The Siddi brothers made Kondaji a sardar in their army. But actually Sambhaji had sent Kondaji and his men to the ammunition storage on the fort in order to capture the fort.

4.2.3 Siege of Janjira

Sambhaji personally attacked Janjira in 1682. He had a 20,000 strong army, 300 ships of the Maratha navy and Maratha artillery assisting him. Maratha admirals Mainak Bhandari, Dariya Sarang and Daulat Khan were commanding the navy. Arab admiral Jange Khan was also helping the Marathas. Siddi forces in the Maratha territories retreated to Janjira fort after seeing such a large army. Sambhaji recaptured the villages surrounding Janjira.

Sambhaji then launched a fierce attack on Janjira. Maratha artillery started to damage the fort walls. The Siddis were also responding strongly with their artillery.

Meanwhile, on the Janjira fort, Kondaji and his men were looking for an opportunity to light the ammunition storage on the fort so as to allow Sambhaji to attack the fort using the ensuing panic on the fort.

300 ships of the Maratha navy were trying to attack the fort but the strong artillery of Siddis somehow managed to defend the fort. Both sides had suffered great losses and nobody was able to gain an upper hand. Sambhaji had maintained a constant pressure on Janjira and his artillery managed to inflict heavy damage to the fort walls. The siege continued for thirty days.

Maratha Navy had blockaded Janjira from three sides cutting of any supplies to the fort. Maratha forces started constructing a bridge from shoreline to the fort. The bridge had started to take shape. Siddis were caught in a dire situation and were battling a severe food shortage. The Siddis realised that if the same situation continues for a few days then Sambhaji will capture the fort in a matter of 4–5 days. Hence they pleaded to Aurangzeb for help.

Aurangzeb was well aware of the strategic importance of Janjira. He immediately sent his General Husain Ali Khan to destroy Kalyan and Bhiwandi regions with a 35,000 strong force to divert Sambhaji's attack on Janjira. Husain Ali Khan destroyed Kalyan and Bhiwandi was threatening to attack Raigad, the Maratha Capital. Sambhaji had almost captured Janjira but he was forced to retreat from Janjira to check Husain Ali Khan's advance. In absence of Sambhaji his naval commander Dadaji Raghunath Deshpande of Mahad took control of the siege. Sambhaji later on defeated and pushed back Husain Ali Khan to Ahmadnagar but Janjira was saved due to his advance on Kalyan-Bhiwandi. Sambhaji was unable to capture the Janjira fort. Nevertheless, he was able to inflict heavy damage to fort. It was an important strategic victory for the Marathas as the Siddis stopped their activities in the Maratha territories and never ventured against the Marathas in Sambhaji's reign.

4.2.4 Aftermath

Siddis had suffered great losses in the siege. They got to know about the superior strength of the Marathas under Sambhaji. They decided not to venture out against the Marathas. In the next few years Aurangzeb repeatedly pleaded them to open a campaign against the Marathas but the Siddis were not ready to fight against the Marathas.

4.3 Battle of Kalyan

The Battle of Kalyan occurred between the Mughal Empire and Maratha Empire between 1682 and 1683. Bahadur Khan of the Mughal Empire defeated the Maratha army and took over Kalyan. The Marathas attempted a counter offensive, but failed and they were repulsed by Mughal forces.

4.4 Siege of Ramsej

Siege of Ramsej (1682-1688) was a series of military confrontations between the Maratha Empire headed by Sambhaji and the Mughal Empire led by Aurangzeb regarding the control of Ramsej Fort in the Nashik region. Aurangzeb arrived in the Deccan in late 1681 with a strong army to destroy the Maratha Empire and the Deccan Sultanates of Adilshahi and Qutubshahi. He wanted to capture the forts held by the Marathas in Nashik and Baglana region. Hence he decided to begin his Deccan campaign with an attack on Ramsej Fort which is near Nashik.

4.4.1 Before the siege

Shivaji's general Moropant Pingle had captured Ramsej in the year 1671-72. Since then, it had been a part of the Maratha Empire. Ramsej was a fort lying in open lands without excessive forest cover. Aurangzeb thought that it would be a good idea to capture an easy fort like Ramsej right at the beginning so as to increase the morale of his troops.

4.4.2 Battles

Ramsej Fort saw the war against the Mughal Empire for six and a half years. The first killedar (fort commander) was Suryaji

Jadhav, but after five and a half years he was transferred and a new killedar was appointed as per the rotation of posts policy of the Maratha Empire. In April 1682, Aurangzeb sent Sahabuddin Khan who attacked the fort. Shahbuddin Khan had vowed to capture the fort with his 40,000 army and strong artillery within a few hours. The Marathas did not succumb to this onslaught. The 600 Maratha soldiers on the fort kept his forces at bay for many months by fierce array of slingshots, lit haystack and huge stones even though they did not have cannons on the fort. Once the Mughal artillery managed to break the fort walls in the evening and they assumed that the fort will be captured easily. But all 600 Marathas on the fort worked for a full night and rebuilt the entire broken section of the wall, much to the despair and awe of the Mughals. Such fierce resistance made the Mughal soldiers believe that the Marathas on the fort knew black magic. The inability of the Mughal Sardar to capture the fort started frustrating Aurangzeb. He raised a wooden platform to storm the fort.

Shivaji and his son Sambhaji had a policy of keeping enough ammunition even on the forts having no cannons or guns. Ramshej was no exception and even though it did not have cannons it had sufficient ammunition. The fort commander had an idea and utilised amply available animal skin and wood on the fort to make wooden cannons. Coupled with the ammunition already present on the fort, these wooden cannons started inflicting heavy losses on the Mughal Army. The retaliation from the Marathas was so strong that he left the responsibility to Bahadur Khan Kokaltash and went to Junnar. Bahadur Khan Kokaltash also tried to capture the fort by fooling Marathas into believing that the Mughals were preparing for a full fledged frontal assault, while his real plan was to send 200 of his best troops from the rear side of the fort by climbing the steep cliff. The Maratha commander was aware of the plan and allowed these 200 soldiers to climb the rope. Once they had climbed up the rope, he cut the rope as a result of which 200 of the best Mughal soldiers fell and died in the valley. Bahadur Khan Kokaltash was distraught and found that Marathas were receiving secret supplies from the nearby forts. He carefully blocked all the paths to nearby Maratha forts. There was dire shortage of food on the fort. Seeing this situation, Maratha King Sambhaji acted quickly by sending his sardars Rupaji Bhosale and Manaji More with an 8,000 strong army and supplies. The two forces clashed at Ganeshgaon. They tried to break through the Mughal line but were unable to supply the fort. Rupaji Bhosale was wounded in the battle. Sambhaji was in great worry that his fiercely brave warriors were fighting without food. One day, due to severe bad weather Bahadur Khan Kokaltash relaxed his encirclement for one day enabling Rupaji Bhosale and Manaji More to supply the fort with supplies enough for 6 more months. Bahadur Khan Kokaltash then tried to win the fort with the help of a 'mantrik' as he believed that the Marathas had ghosts under their control. The Marathas again fooled him as the mantrik was himself a Maratha soldier in disguise who led the Mughal Army in a deadly ambush of the Marathas. Bahadur Khan Kokaltash and Mughals fled the deadly ambush and several Mughals were killed in this surprise attack. Bahadur Khan Kokaltash was also unable to siege the fort, finally, he burnt the wooden platform and left the battle.

The frustrated Aurangzeb then sent Kasim Khan Kirmani to lead the battle and Kasim Khan finally decided to lead the 36,500 strong Mughal soldiers right into the fort with an all-out assault.

So, the Mughal soldiers finally stormed Ramsej Fort and killed many Maratha soldiers. However, many of the Marathas escaped capture or death by using a rope which had been set by Rupaji Bhosale from the back-windows of the fort. Thus, many Marathas managed to escape before the Mughals finally took control of the fort. Finally, the Mughals hoisted their imperial flag atop the fort and the fort was finally taken after a long, hard, and tiring 6 years.

4.5 Maratha-Mysore War (1682)

The Maratha-Mysore War (1682) refers to a series of battles fought between the Maratha Empire and the Kingdom of Mysore in Southern India, both of which were attempting to establish supremacy in Southern India. The Maratha forces were led by Sambhaji and the Mysore forces were led by Chikka Devaraja. The conflict resulted in the defeat of the Mysore Forces at the hands of the Marathas, leading to a conclusion at the Treaty of Srirangapatanam (also called Srirangapatinam or Srirangapatna).

4.5.1 Background

Sambhaji's grandfather, Shahaji, had conquered territories in the states of Karnataka, leading to Mohammed Adil Shah, Sultan of Bijapur granting him the title of Jagir of Bangalore. These events began the entry of the Marathas in the Southern India. Shivaji had established Maratha territories in the Southern India in his two-year-long campaign of 1676–78. The Maratha Empire and the Mysore kingdom were the main contenders to dominate the region, and the relationship between the two was generally hostile. In 1681, the Marathas attacked Srirangapatna, but were defeated, though the Maratha Sardar Harji Raje Mahadik defeated the Mysore general Kumaraiya. Both forces had tried to subdue each other resulting in a stalemate. Sambhaji also tried to form a Deccan alliance against the Mughal Emperor Aurangzeb. Chikkadevaraya allied himself with Aurangzeb and executed the Maratha generals Dadaji Kakade, Jaitaji Katkar and Santaji Nimbalkar. This enraged Sambhaji and he attacked the Kingdom of Mysore in June 1682 with his allies Qutb Shahi dynasty and the Nayakas of Hukkeri. Allied forces reached Banavar in June 1682.

4.5.2 Battle of Banavar

To counter the allied army at Banavar, Chikkadevaraya left Mysore with his strong contingent of 15,000 expert archers. He wanted to attack before thc allies settled in the region. Both sides prepared for the battle. And the battle began with small skirmishes.

Soon, Chikkadevaraya realised that the allied forces did not have archers. He arranged his archers in a semicircular formation and started showering arrows on the allied army. The Marathas did not expect this and the arrows started mounting casualties In the allied army. Maratha commanders tried but were unable to stop the rout. Some more reinforcements joined the Marathas during the battle, but they suffered heavy casualties in the battle. The Mysore archers took a break for dinner in the night. Sambhaji decided to retreat to avoid more casualties and he retreated towards Thanjavur.

4.5.3 Battle of Trichinopoly

Sambhaji rested near Thanjavur for 20 days. He received more reinforcements from Hukkeri and Golconda. His uncle Ekoji I also joined forces with him.

Sambhaji had realized the strength of Mysore forces near their heartland. He decided to draw them away from their stronghold to flat plains near Madurai. He decided to attack and besiege the city of Tiruchirapalli.

The weakened Nayaka of Madurai, Chokkanatha Nayak lived on the fort. He was a vassal of the Kingdom of Mysore. Still, the city had strong defences and a formidable Mysore garrison in the city and on the fort.

Sambhaji wanted to negate the superiority of Mysore archers. During their rest time Sambhaji ordered all the cobblers from neighbouring villages and made leather arrow-proof jackets for his entire army. These leather jackets were coated with a layer of oil to avoid arrows from getting stuck in the jackets. Sambhaji also collected the abundantly available war elephants from the surrounding region. He ordered all the boatmen from the nearby villages to assemble with his army. 300 archers of the Maratha army were prepared to fire lit arrows during the attack.

Tiruchirapalli lied on the opposite bank of the Kaveri river. At the dawn, the Maratha forces crossed the river using the boats collected from nearby villages. The sudden attack of the Marathas surprised the Mysore defenders, they started showering arrows on the Maratha Army. The Maratha leather jackets provided effective protection and negated arrows from the Mysore bowmen. Elephants broke through the main doors in the meanwhile and fierce battle ensued on the streets of Tiruchirappalli. Marathas captured the city by the evening but the Tiruchirapalli Rock Fort was still controlled by the Mysore army.

Meanwhile Chokkanatha Nayak died on the fort. Sambhaji with a force of 10,000 laid siege to the fort after 10 days. The Marathas again adopted similar tactics to negate Mysore archers. The Maratha archers accurately struck lit arrows on the ammunitions depot within the fort resulting in a huge explosion, and collapse of the wall. The Marathas soon entered and captured the fort. The Marathas sacked Tiruchirapalli.

Historian Sadashiv Shivde has mentioned that, this victory was a success point of Sambhaji's military intelligence.

4.5.4 Aftermath

The defeat at Trichinopoly (Tiruchirappalli) dealt a severe blow to Chikkadevaraya. Several of his allies joined Sambhaji. Sambhaji captured several fortresses in the northern provinces of Madurai. He also held all the province of Dharmapuri and other neighbouring territories. Chikkadevaraya entered negotiations with Sambhaji and brought an end to the war by paying the tribute. According to Maratha sources a treaty was signed at Srirangapatna in which he paid 1 Crore Honas as a war tribute to Sambhaji. However this was a temporary surrender and the conflicts continued in the following years. The Jesuit letter of 1682 describes the precarious position of Chikka Devaraja, 'The power of the king of Mysore begins to grow weak because, violently attacked in his own dominions by the troops of Sambhaji, he cannot sustain and reinforce the armies he had sent to those countries.'

4.6 Maratha invasion of Goa (1683)

Maratha Invasion of Goa (1683) or Sambhaji's Invasion of Goa refers to the invasion of Portuguese controlled portion of contemporary Goa and the northern areas of Konkan. The battles were fought between the Mahratta Confederacy and the Portuguese in Goa and Bombay-Bassein, on various fronts in between 1682-1683.

In 1682, 2 years after the death of Shivaji, Marathas began arming and fortifying their border with Portuguese held territories, and the Portuguese increasingly allied themselves with the Moghul empire to avert the looming threat, this would set the background for a series of Mahratta hostilities in and around the present-day Goa and Bombay of the Konkan region.

The Ponda Fort near the capital city of Velha Goa was a strategic Maratha position, hence the viceroy Francisco led a botched attack on it in late 1683, attempting to avert the Mahratta threat to the Portuguese capital. Sambhaji arrived with reinforcements and tried to press on the advantage of the Portuguese retreat at Ponda. He stormed the colony of Goa, Marathas temporarily occupied many forts in Goa. The Maratha forces were preemptively mobilised, and the Portuguese situation eventually became dire. Sambhaji ransacked the north Konkan region for over a month, his forces also pillaged Salcette and Bardes areas in south Konkan. Sambhaji came very close to capturing the city of Old Goa, but his forces retreated from Goa, Damaon& Diu and the northern areas of Konkan division on 2 January 1684, to avoid the large Moghul army led by Prince Muazzam (alias Bahadur Shah I).

4.6.1 Background

The Portuguese Empire was a powerful naval empire in the 17th century. They had established several enclaves on the west coast of India. The Portuguese territories of Damaon, Chaul, Bacaim, Goa and several others, bordered the Maratha Empire. The Marathas during the lifetime of Shivaji had maintained relatively good relations with the Portuguese East Indies. His successor, Sambhaji wanted to check up the Portuguese by constructing forts over at strategic locations, one being Anjediva Island off the coast of modern-day North Canara, and another on Parsik Hill in modern-day New Bombay. The Portuguese were alarmed at the mobilisation of Maratha forces and fortification at the borders, and attempted to stop the construction of the forts in 1683. In August 1683, the Portuguese allowed the Mughal army to pass through their northern territories against the Marathas. When Sambhaji received information about Mughal-Portuguese cooperation. He adopted an aggressive strategy by attacking the villages of Chaul, Bacaim and Daman. The Marathas then plundered Portuguese controlled villages in Dahanu, Asheri and Bacaim. In response the Portuguese arrested the Maratha envoy Yesaji Gambhir. Sambhaji's Peshwa Nilopant Pingle waged aggressive war against the Portuguese. He devastated, plundered& occupied 40 miles of Portuguese territory including the villages of Chembur, Talode, Kolve, Mahim, Dantore, Sargaon. The Portuguese retaliated by arresting Maratha merchant ships. They also attacked the newly built fort on Parsik Hill. All these events took place in April–May 1683. The Marathas also besieged Revdanda fort and plundered its village in July 1683. The Portuguese Viceroy Francisco de Távora, wanted the capture of Sambhaji. Desai Brahmins of Sawantwadi sided with the

Portuguese in this conflict, as they lost most of their political privileges under the Maratha rule.

4.6.2 Battle of Ponda Fort

The Portuguese viceroy marched towards the Fortress of Ponda, with 3,700 soldiers. Viceroy camped at the border village of Agaçaim on 27 October 1683. They crossed the river and reached the villages west of Ponda on 7 November. Veteran Maratha general Yesaji Kank and his son Krishnaji were stationed at Ponda with a force of 600 Mavalas. The Marathas resisted the initial Portuguese infantry charges. In one of these skirmishes Krishnaji Kank was wounded heavily, he died a few days later. However The Portuguese heavy bombardment managed to broke through the walls of the fort, severely damaging it.

By 9 November Maratha reinforcements, which included Sambhaji himself, arrived from Rajapur to rescue the fort. He had 800 cavalry and 2,000 infantry with him. Viceroy thought that Sambhaji will attack him from the rear and cut his line of communication with Goa. On 10 November, he called for a general retreat towards the Durbhat port. The Marathas routed the retreating Portuguese by attacking them from a hill near creek. The viceroy was wounded during this skirmish. On 12 November most of the Portuguese army reached Goa. This victory of Sambhaji has been praised by the Portuguese and they described Sambhaji as a war like prince.

4.6.3 Invasion of Goa

In the north, the Peshva Brahmin leader by the name Nilopant Pingle kept pressure on Revdanda. The Marathas also temporarily occupied some territory around Bassein and

Damaon. The viceroy had assumed that Sambhaji would quit the heavily damaged Ponda and leave, to the inland Panhala Fort.

On 24 November 1683 at night, when the tide was low, Sambhaji's full force attacked the unsuspecting fort and village on St Estevam island. They captured the fort and plundered its village. A battalion of 200 men marched from Goan capital in order to recapture the island. Seeing the size of the Maratha army, and the devastation caused by them, the battalion retreated to the capital city of Goa.

After the fall of St Estêvão, and arrival of the retreating army, the Portuguese broke the bunds of rice fields on the outskirts of the city of Goa. This inundated the fields with river water, the plan worked by increasing the width of the river. Sambhaji had intended to raid Goa but was prevented by the rising tide combined with the flood from rice fields. The Marathas later retreated from the island due to the probability of a Portuguese naval attack.

News reached both Sambhaji and the viceroy, that a Mughal prince, Muazzam, had entered into Maratha territory with a 100,000 strong force. The Moghuls took advantage of Sambhaji's war with the Portuguese as a diversion. Sambhaji tried to bribe Muazzam to get him to use his army against the Portuguese before Moghuls could reach south Konkani city of Goa. With this failing, Sambhaji continued storming the northern parts of the colony, attacking poorly defended villages. By December 1683, the Maratha force had been reinforced and totalled to 6,000 cavalry and 8,000 - 10,000 infantry units. They attacked the areas of Salcette and Bardes and plundered town of Margão. The Portuguese successfully defended the inner territories of Ilhas de

Goa and Mormugão from the onslaught of Marathas. All the other villages and forts were temporarily occupied by the Marathas. French factor of Surat Francois Martin has described the poor condition of the Portuguese, he said the viceroy was completely dependent on Moghul aid now. After having laying waste to the outer districts of Salcete and Bardez the Marathas and had started closing in to the Islands of Goa. The viceroy was concerned that if the things remain unchanged, Sambhaji would soon capture the island of Goa. During this time, Muazzam was pillaging through the Maratha territory, as he made his approach towards Sambhaji. When Sambhaji learnt of Muazzam's arrival at Ramghat, fearing the large Moghul army he retreated all his forces back to Raigad Fort on 2 January 1684.

It is said that the viceroy went to the body of Francis Xavier, in the Bom Jesus shrine in the Velha Goa city, and placed his sceptre on the dead saint's relic and prayed for his grace to avert the Mahratta threat. The belief that Francis Xavier had saved the Portuguese led to the celebration of this occasion annually in Goa.

4.6.4 Aftermath

Sambhaji wanted peace with the Portuguese, as he was unable to fight a war on two fronts. He sent Prince Akbar and Kavi Kalash to negotiate with the Portuguese. After long negotiations final treaty was approved at Mardangad, between 25 January and 4 February.

Due to the arrival of Portuguese reinforcements in Goa and the Konkan, the Marathas realized that they were not going to be able to continue their conquest against the Portuguese, or keep any of their territories. The Marathas retreated from all their new possessions, in order to concentrate their forces against the Mughals. The campaign was a reality check for Portuguese aspirations in the Konkan. On 12 January 1684, the viceroy called a meeting of the state council to shift the capital Goa to Mormugao fortress further West. This proposal was rejected, and the capital continued to be the Old Goa. The viceroy did not expect hostile actions from the Marathas, until he met Sambhaji on the battlefield. In spite of the fact that Goa was well fortified and the Portuguese had a fine navy. The conflicts between the two powers continued in the following years, as Marathas continued raiding the borders, culminating in the Mahratta Invasion of Bassein, the Portuguese however did not make any significant offensive campaigns against the Marathas.

4.7 Mughal invasions of Konkan (1684)

Mughal invasion of Konkan (1684) was a part of the Deccan wars. It was a campaign launched by Mughal Emperor Aurangzeb to capture the Konkan region from the Maratha Empire under Sambhaji. The Mughal forces were led by Mu'azzam and Shahbuddin Khan. The harsh climate and the Maratha guerrilla strategy forced the numerically strong Mughal army into a slow retreat. The Mughal army suffered significant losses in this unsuccessful campaign.

4.7.1 Background

Aurangzeb tried attacking the Maratha Empire from all directions, intending to use the Mughal numerical superiority to his advantage. Sambhaji had prepared well for the invasions and the Maratha forces promptly engaged the numerically strong Mughal army in several small battles using guerrilla warfare tactics. However, Sambhaji and his generals attacked and Defeated the Mughal generals whenever they got an opportunity to lure the Mughal generals into decisive battles in the Maratha stronghold territories. Sambhaji had devised a strategy of minimising the losses on his side. If there used to be an opportunity then the Maratha army attacked decisively if the Mughals were too strong in numbers then the Marathas used to retreat. This proved to be a very effective strategy as Aurangzeb's generals were not able capture the Maratha territories for three years continuously. He then decided to attack the Maratha capital Raigad Fort directly from the north and south. He made a pincer attempt to surround the Maratha Capital that led to Mughal invasions of Konkan (1684).

4.7.2 Preparations

In late 1683, Sambhaji thrashed and put pressure on the Portuguese in Goa and Bombay-Bassein, in a campaign known as Sambhaji's invasion of Goa (1683). Goa was almost captured and the viceroy of Goa asked Aurangzeb for immediate help. At this same time Aurangzeb devised a grand pincer attempt to attack the Maratha capital at Raigad Fort from the North and the South. He sent his general Shahbuddin Khan to attack Raigad via north Konkan from his position in the Guzerati subah. The other Mughal flank was led by Prince Muazzam with a 1,00,000 strong force. His army consisted of 40,000 horsemen, 60,000 foot, 1,900 elephants and 2,000 camels. Prince Muazzam (Shah Alam) was to win the South Konkan, Ramdara and other territories of Maratha's. Muazzam was provided with a huge army of brave and famous sardars like Atishkhan (artillery inspector), Latifshah, Sarfarzkhan, Ikhlaskhan, Nagoji (he knew the territory very well). Originally, Muazzam had a 45,000 force under his command. Hasan Ali Khan who was at bank of river Bhima was ordered to join forces with Muazzam. There were short battles between Maratha forces and leading forces of the Mughal army. The Mughals lost and fled. Then Mughal force attacked Sampgad (fort of Sampgaon) and seized the fort where their two-three famous sardars were injured.

Both Sambhaji and viceroy had information that Mughal prince Muazzam is coming to the aid of Portuguese with a 1,00,000 strong force. Sambhaji decided to make use of his army against the Portuguese before the Mughal army could reach South Konkan. Sambhaji stormed the colony taking its forts. On 11 December 1683, Sambhaji's army attacked Salsette and Bardez. Sambhaji had 6 thousand cavalry and 8-10 thousand infantry with him. Marathas plundered Bardesh and town of Madgaon. The Portuguese successfully defended only Aguada, Reis-Magos, Raitur and Murgao forts against the onslaught of Marathas. All the other forts were captured by the Marathas. French factor of Surat Francois Martin has described the poor condition of the Portuguese, he said the viceroy was completely dependent on Mughal aid now.

After having captured Salsette and Bardesh (Bardez) the Marathas were exerting to take the island of Goa as well. The viceroy feared if the things remain unchanged, Sambhaji would soon conquer the island of Goa. He went to the body of St. Francis Xavier, lying in the Bom Jesus church in old Goa, and placed his sceptre on the dead saint's hand and prayed for his grace to avert the Maratha threat. When Sambhaji learnt of

Muazzam's approach from Ramghat which is just 30 miles from Goa, he withdrew all his forces to Raigad on 2 January 1684. Sambhaji didn't want to get trapped between Portuguese and Mughal armies, hence he decided to adopt a defensive strategy. Orleans said that Sambhaji didn't consider himself strong enough to resist such huge number and thought of securing safety by a masterly retreat which he affected so cleverly that he retired to his fastness before mogul could engage him". Sambhaji very quickly and cleverly retreated home before Mughals could attack him. After returning home Sambhaji had an idea of the huge force of Muazzam, hence to face his large army Sambhaji started to increase strength of his army.

Aurangzeb had also sent Shahbuddin Khan to attack Raigad via North Konkan.

4.7.3 Events in the campaign

On 28 December 1683 Muazzam burned down the towns of Kudal and Bande. On 15 January 1684 he burned down Dicholi, forces of Muazzam destroyed temples, looted the port of Vengurla. The Mughal forces faced severe food shortage, his soldiers were starving, hence he ordered Khairatkhan and Yakutkhan of Surat to send him food supplies. Muazzam asked for permission to pass his ships carrying food which was granted by Portuguese. The Portuguese sent a lawyer to Muzzam requesting Alam not to retreat from Konkan and keep fighting against Sambhaji, Portuguese who had lost more than 20 lakh rupees due to war with Maratha. Still he was demanding this same amount and 600 horses and the Konkan territory from Banda to Mirjan. However, no such deal took place in reality because the ships carrying food supplies sent to Muazzam did not reach Goa because, different Maratha sea-fort commanders attacked and captured them when they received information about these ships. Only a few ships escaped but they did not carry enough food supplies. Muazzam was ordered to return from Konkan. Muazzam decided to leave Konkan before rainy season. On their way back, the Mughal army suffered much (while going through Ramghat) due to scarcity of food, constant attacks of Marathas, and diseases. When Muazzam crossed the Ramghat, he was left with little cavalry, the Marathas were constantly attacking him from all sides using guerilla tactics. Mughal sardar Bahadur Khan met Muazzam and provided him with equipment and force. In April–May of 1684 Muazzam stayed at shakes/sheks village near Bijapur, in the month of June he reached at Bank of river Bhima where he had battle with 5000 Maratha forces and he was injured in that battle. The expedition of Konkan by Muazzam was big failure as the Mughals lost 60,000 soldiers, hundreds of camels, artillery pieces, lakhs of rupees, for virtually no success.

After the 1684 monsoon, Aurangzeb's other general Shahbuddin Khan directly attacked the Maratha capital, Raigad. Maratha commanders successfully defended Raigad. Aurangzeb sent Khan Jehan to help, but Hambirrao Mohite, commander-in-chief of the Maratha army, defeated him in a fierce battle at Patadi. The second division of the Maratha army attacked Shahbuddin Khan at Pachad, inflicting heavy losses on the Mughal army.

4.7.4 Aftermath and consequences

The campaign had various political and military consequences.

4.7.4.1 Military consequences

1) Aurangzeb had sent his son Bahadur Shah I, and other great nobles on this invasion. This invasion lasted from 20 August 1683 to 24 May 1684. There were few incidents of actual fighting. At the end of the battle, the situation remained the same. Only the main road between Nizampur and Ramghat to Vengurla was destroyed. By this time the crops had been removed. There was no question of looting as there was no other place in Pethe except Sampagava. The dew did not cause much damage to the village even before the invasion.

4.7.4.2 The effects of this invasion on politics were:

1. The Portuguese who were inclined towards the Mughals due to Sambhaji's invasion were annoyed by the plunder of Bardesh by the people of Shah Alam and the destruction of the Mughal Armory caravan and the looting . He insisted on concluding a pact with Sambhaji. The Mughals lost a friend as it was their interest to depend on Sambhaji.

2. Seeing the misery of the Portuguese and considering the struggle of the Mughal emperor, it was in their interest to hold on to Sambhaji. Also, the arson and looting of Sambhaji in the region near Mumbai was stopped.

3. Taking advantage of the animosity between the Portuguese and the Arabs, Sambhaji befriended the Arabs, and with the support of Arabs Chhatrapati Sambhaji Maharaj's navy became stronger.

4. The Adilshahi king was persuaded to side Sambhaji was able to make a pact with them. Hence an alliance of Adilashahi-Marathas-Qutbshahi was formed.

The mughal ships suffered heavy losses only for the transportation of grain. Much of the grain supply fell into the hands of Sambhaji and some sank in the sea. So Shah Alam had to return and there was a famine in Surat.

In summary, the Mughals were defeated even though they marched with a force of one lakh and ran hundreds of miles without encountering a real enemy.

4.8 Battle of Wai

The Battle of Wai was fought in the fall of 1687 as a part of the Mughal–Maratha Wars. Sambhaji sent his forces under his senapati, Hambirao Mohite, to oppose Mughal army led by Sarja Khan. The Mughal's were drawn into the dense jungles near Wai and Mahableshwar where the battle ensued and the Marathas were eventually victorious.

4.8.1 Background

In April 1685, Mughal emperor Aurangzeb managed to consolidate his power by first capturing Maratha allies, the Muslim kingdoms of Golkonda and Bijapur. He broke his treaties with both kingdoms, attacked them and captured them by September 1686. While Aurangzeb was away at the Siege of Golconda, the Mughals invaded Satara district. And after his victory at Golconda, Aurangzeb was able to concentrate on the Marathas.

4.8.2 Battle

Maratha Empire senapati, or general, Sardar Hambirao Mohite (Talbeed) led the Maratha side in the battle. Sarja Khan (a Bijapur general who has joined the Mughel's) led the Mughal force. The Mughals were defeated but Hambirao Mohite was struck and killed by a cannonball during the battle. The Samadhi of this Hambirrao Mohite is located somewhere on the banks of river Krishna in Wai taluka (Satara district).

4.8.3 Aftermath

While the battle was a victory for the Maratha's, the loss of the celebrated Hambirao Mohite weakened Sambhaji's political position considerably and many of his troops deserted him. Hambirao was replaced as senapati by Malhoji Ghorpade. Sambhaji went to the Western Ghats along with his close friend and counselor Kavi Kalash, leading eventually to the Mughal Army surrounding the Sambhaji's camp and capturing the Maratha leader.

CHAPTER 5

Battles under Peshwa Baji Rao Ballal I

5.1 Battle of Palkhed

Palkhed Battle field Location

The Battle of Palkhed was fought on February 28, 1728 at the village of Palkhed, near the city of Nashik, Maharashtra, India between the Maratha Empire and the Nizam-ul-Mulk, Asaf Jah I of Hyderabad wherein, the Marathas defeated the Nizam.

5.1.1 Background

The seeds of this battle go to the year 1713, when Maratha king Shahu, appointed Balaji Vishwanath as his *Peshwa* or Prime Minister. Within a decade, Balaji had managed to extract a significant amount of territory and wealth from the fragmenting Mughal Empire. In 1724, Mughal control lapsed, and Asaf Jah I, the 1st Nizam of Hyderabad declared himself independent of Mughal rule, thereby establishing his own kingdom known as Hyderabad Deccan.

The Nizam set about strengthening the province by attempting to control the growing influence of the Marathas.

He utilized a growing polarization in the Maratha Empire due to the claim of the title of King by both Shahu and Sambhaji II of Kolhapur. The Nizam began supporting the Sambhaji II faction, which enraged Shahu who had been proclaimed as King. The Nizam further decided to halt Chauth given by many landowners of the Deccan province to the Marathas, as had been agreed by the Syed Brothers in 1719.

5.1.2 Prelude

The battle plan was set by the withdrawal of Baji Rao's army from the southern reaches of the Maratha empire during May 1727. This was followed by Shahu breaking off negotiations with the Nizam-ul-Mulk about the restoration of the Chauth.

Troop movements of Baji Rao I and Nizam-ul-Mulk before the Battle of Palkhed

The Nizam pursued Baji Rao's army around the vicinity of Pune for about six months, where Baji Rao executed a series of thrust and parry moves to finally corner the Nizam at Palkhed.

5.1.2.1 The Battles

Baji Rao and the Maratha armies were called back from the south, from the Karnataka campaign. In May 1727, Baji Rao then asked Shahu to break off negotiations with Nizam-ul-Mulk, Asaf Jah I (Nizam-ul-Mulk had called for arbitration over the payment of the Chauth and sardeshmukhi) and started mobilizing an army. With the monsoons over and the land ready for this exciting campaign, Baji Rao moved towards Aurangabad.

After a skirmish near Jalna (the Marathas by now had become famous for their strategy of not engaging with the enemy) with Iwaz Khan (the General of Nizam-ul-Mulk), as could have been predicted, Baji Rao moved away from the battlefield, towards Burhanpur.

Nizam-ul-Mulk's army pursued Baji Rao. Baji Rao then moved westwards to Gujarat from North Khandesh. However, the Nizam-ul-Mulk gave up the pursuit and moved southward towards Pune. This is an interesting reason and comparison between how the two armies functioned. The Nizam is known to have carried huge armies with him, including supplies to last for the duration of the campaign. In fact, the Nizam used to carry his jenana or womenfolk with him during his campaigns. The Maratha armies, however, were very light and found supplies on the way by plundering and looting outposts on the way.

As Nizam-ul-Mulk left the pursuit of Baji Rao and moved towards the headquarters of the Shahu stronghold, posts like Udaipur, Avasari, Pabal, Khed, and Narayangarh surrendered to Nizam-ul-Mulk, who then occupied Pune and advanced towards Supa, Patas, and Baramati.

5.1.2.2 Sambhaji II's Withdrawal

In Baramati, Nizam-ul-Mulk got news of Baji Rao moving towards Aurangabad. Nizam-ul-Mulk began moving northwards to intercept the Maratha Army. By this time he was confident of crushing Baji Rao and his army. It was not to happen so. The Raja of Kolhapur, Sambhaji II refused to join him in this campaign against Baji Rao. The Nizam was cornered in a waterless tract near Palkhed on 25 February 1728. Through Iwaz Khan, the Nizam-ul-Mulk sent out a word of his plight, and his army was allowed to move to the vicinity of the river. The Mughal emperor Farrukhsiyar appointed Nizam-ul-Mulk as Subedar of Deccan.

5.1.3 Outcome

The Nizam of Hyderabad was defeated by the Marathas, and Peshwa Baji Rao I made him sign a peace treaty on 6 March 1728 at the village of Mungi-Paithan.

By the treaty of Munji Shivagaon, the Nizam agreed to make certain concessions to the Peshwa.

Chhatrapati Shahu was recognised as the sole Maratha ruler.

Marathas were given the right to collect Chauth and Sardeshmukhi of Deccan.

Those revenue collectors driven out would be reappointed.

The balance revenue was to be paid to Chhatrapati Shahu.

5.2 Battle of Bundelkhand

The Battle of Jaitpur was fought between the Maratha Empire under Peshwa Baji Rao I, on behalf of Chhatrasal Bundela, the ruler of Bundelkhand; and the Mughal empire under of Muhammad Khan Bangash in March 1729. Bangash attacked the state of Bundelkhand in December 1728. Being too old to fight, as well as heavily outnumbered, Chhatrasal appealed Baji Rao for assistance- under whose leadership the Maratha-Bundela alliance defeated Bangash at Jaitpur.

5.2.1 Background

In Bundelkhand, Chhatrasal had rebelled against the Mughal Empire and established an independent kingdom. In December 1728, a Mughal force led by Muhammad Khan Bangash attacked him and besieged his fort and family. Although Chhatrasal repeatedly sought Baji Rao's assistance, he was busy in Malwa at the time. He compared his dire situation to that of Gajendra Moksha. In his letter to Baji Rao, Chhatrasal wrote the following words:

Know you, that I am in the same sad plight in which the famous elephant was when caught by the crocodile. My valiant race is on point of extinction. Come and save my honour, O Baji Rao.

5.2.2 Battle

In March 1729, the Peshwa responded to Chhatrasal's request and marched towards Bundelkhand with 25,000 horsemen and his lieutenants Pilaji Jadhav, Tukoji Pawar, Naro Shankar, Ramsingha and Davalji Somwanshi. Chhatrasal escaped capture and joined the Maratha force, increasing it to 70,000 men. After marching to Jaitpur, Baji Rao's forces surrounded Bangash and cut his supply and communication lines. Bangash launched a counterattack against Baji Rao, but could not pierce his defences. Qaim Khan, son of Muhammad Khan Bangash, learned of his father's predicament and approached with fresh troops. His army was attacked by Baji Rao's forces, and he was defeated. Bangash was later forced to leave, signing an agreement that "he would never attack Bundelkhand again".

5.2.3 Aftermath

Chhatrasal's position as ruler of Bundelkhand was restored. He granted a large jagir to Baji Rao, and gave him his daughter from a concubine named Ruhani Bai, Mastani. Before Chhatrasal's death in December 1731, he ceded one-third of his territories to the Marathas.

5.3 Battle of Dabhoi

Battle of Dabhoi was a major confrontation between the Mughal Empire's Maratha Faction and Baji Rao I and Chimnaji Appa.

5.3.1 Background

In the year 1731, Asaf Jah I the Nizam of Hyderabad had managed to secure the defections of influential Maratha leaders such as Trimbak Rao Dabhade and Sanbhoji who threatened to abandon the Marathas and join the forces with the Mughal Emperor Muhammad Shah instead.

5.3.2 Battle

This move was considered unacceptable by Baji Rao I and his brother Chimnaji Appa who led a large well armed brigade of Marathas to intercepte Trimbak Rao Dabhade and Sanbhoji during the Battle of Dabhoi, where the defecting factions were all defeated, overrun and eliminated.

5.3.3 Aftermath

Baji Rao I then attacked Gujarat with full force and finally drove out Sarbuland Khan by 1735.

5.4 Battle of Mandsaur

The Battle of Mandsaur took place in Mandsaur, modern day Madhya Pradesh between Marathas, commanded by Malharrao Holkar, and Jai Singh of Amber, in which Jai Singh was defeated in February, 1733. Malhar Rao Holkar then conquered Bundelkhand and Bundi.

5.5 Battle of Delhi (1737)

The battle took place on 28 March 1737 between the Marathas and the Mughal Empire at Talkatora near Delhi. It was part of the Later Mughal-Maratha Wars (1728–1763).

5.5.1 Background

On 12 November 1736, the Maratha general Bajirao advanced on Old Delhi to attack the Mughal capital. Mughal emperor Muhammad Shah sent Saadat Ali Khan I with a 150,000-strong army to stop the Maratha advance on Delhi. But Bajirao's subordinate chiefs Malhar Rao Holkar and Pilaji Jadhav crossed the river Yamuna and looted Ganga-Yamuna Doab, Saadat Khan defeated the maratha forces under Malhar Rao and retired to Mathura. Bajirao's army advanced to Delhi and encamped near Talkatora.

5.5.2 Battle

Muhammad Shah sent Mir Hasan Khan Koka with an army to intercept Bajirao. The Mughals led an attack on Maratha army but were repulsed with heavy losses.

5.5.3 Aftermath

The battle signified the further expansion of the Maratha Empire towards the north. Muhammad Shah called upon the Nizam's and Nawab's armies to destroy the Maratha Army. The Nizam of Hyderabad and the Nawab of Bhopal left Hyderabad to protect the Mughal Empire from the invasion of the Marathas, but they were defeated decisively in the Battle of Bhopal (24 December 1737). The Marathas extracted large tributaries from the Mughals, and signed a treaty which ceded Malwa to the Marathas.

The Maratha plunder weakened the Mughal Empire, which got further weakened after successive invasions of Nadir Shah in 1739 and Ahmad Shah Abdali in the 1750s. The continuous attacks led the Marathas to wage another Battle of Delhi in 1757 against the Rohillas who were pushed out, which largely effaced the remaining central authority of the Mughal Empire.

5.6 Battle of Bhopal

The Battle of Bhopal, was fought on 24 December 1737 in Bhopal between the Maratha Empire and the combined army of the Nizam and several Mughal generals.

5.6.1 Background

As the Mughal empire continued to weaken after Aurangzeb's death, the Maratha Peshwa Bajirao I invaded Mughal territories such as Malwa and Gujarat. The Mughal emperor was alarmed by Marathas conquest. In 1737, the Marathas invaded the northern frontiers of the Mughal empire, reaching as far as the outskirts of Delhi, Bajirao defeated a Mughal army there and was marching back to Pune.

The Mughal emperor asked for support from the Nizam. The Nizam intercepted the Marathas during the latter's return journey. The two armies clashed near Bhopal.

5.6.2 Battle

The battle was fought between the Maratha Empire and Mughal forces led by Nizam of Hyderabad near Bhopal in India in December 1737. The Marathas poisoned the water and the replenishment supplies of the besieged Mughal forces. Chimaji was sent with an army of 10,000 men to stop any reinforcements while Bajirao blockaded the city instead of directly attacking the Nizam. The Nizam was forced to sue for peace after he was denied reinforcements from Delhi. The battle resulted in Maratha victory mainly because of the swift tactics of Maratha Peshwa Baji Rao.

5.6.3 Aftermath

Later, on 7 January 1738, a peace treaty was signed between Peshwa Bajirao and Jai Singh II, in Doraha near Bhopal. Marathas were given the territory of Malwa

5.7 Battle of Vasai

The Battle of Vasai or the Battle of Bassein was fought between the Marathas and the Portuguese rulers of Vasai (Portuguese, Baçaim; English, Bassein), a town lying near Mumbai (Bombay) in the Konkan region of present-day state of Maharashtra, India. The Marathas were led by Chimaji Appa, a brother of Peshwa Baji Rao I. Maratha victory in this war was a major achievement of Baji Rao I's reign.

5.7.1 Background

The *Provincia do Norte* (Province of the North) region ruled by the Portuguese included not just the town of Baçaim but also areas   far   away as Bombay, Thana, Kalyan, Chaul and Revdanda. Baçaim is located about 50 kilometers north of Bombay, on the Arabian Sea. Baçaim, was an important trading center, and its sources of wealth was trade in horses, fish, salt, timber, basalt and granite, as well as shipbuilding. The town was a significant trading center long before the Portuguese arrived. Ancient Sopara was an important port that traded with the Arabs and Greeks, Romans and Persians. It was also a wealthy agricultural region with rice, betel nut, cotton, and sugar-cane widely grown.

5.7.2 16th Century

In 1530, Portuguese army captain António da Silveira burnt the city of Baçaim and continued the burning and looting up to nearby Bombaim, when the King of Thana surrendered islands of Mahim and Bombaim.   Subsequently,   the   towns of Thana, Bandora, Mahim and Bombaim (Bombay)   were brought under Portuguese control. In 1531, António de Saldanha while returning from Gujarat to Goa, set fire to Baçaim again — to punish Sultanate of Gujarat king Bahadur Shah for not ceding Diu.

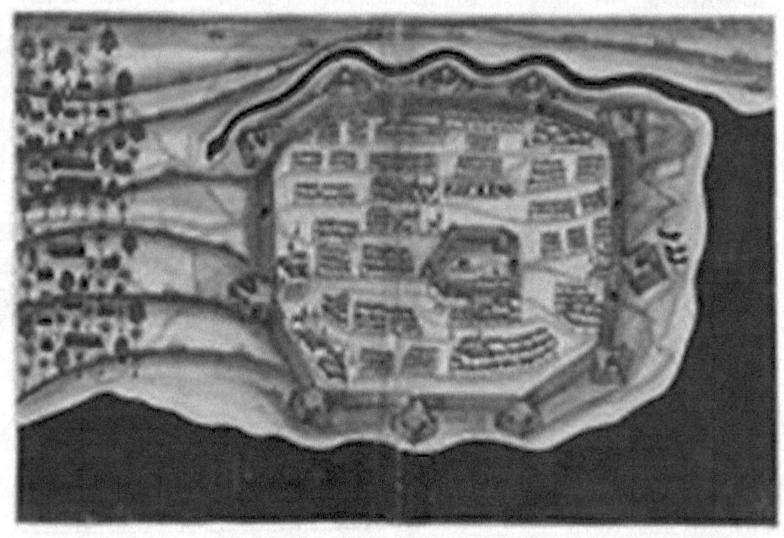

Plant of the Baçaim Fortress (1635)

In 1533, Diogo (Heytor) de Sylveira, burnt the entire sea coast from Bandora, Thana, Baçaim, to Surat. Diogo de Sylveira returned to Goa with 4000 slaves and spoils of pillaging. For the Portuguese, Diu was an important island to protect their trade, which they had to capture. While devising the means to capture Diu, Portuguese General Nuno da Cunha, found out that the governor of Diu was Malik Ayaz whose son Malik Tokan was fortifying Baçaim with 14,000 men.

Engraving depicting Antonio Galvano (c.1490–1557)

Nuno da Cunha saw this fortification as a threat. He assembled a fleet of 150 ships with 4000 men and sailed to Baçaim. Upon seeing such a formidable naval power, Malik Tokan made overtures of peace to Nuno da Cunha. The peace overtures were rejected. Malik Tokan had no option but to fight the Portuguese. The Portuguese landed north of the Baçaim and invaded the fortification. Even though the Portuguese were numerically insignificant, they fought with skill and valor killing off most of the enemy soldiers while losing only a handful of their own.

Portrait of Nuno da Cunha

On 23 December 1534, the Sultan of Gujarat Bahadur Shah, signed a treaty with the Portuguese and ceded Baçaim with its dependencies of Salsette,Bombaim(Bombay), Parel, Vadala, Siao (Sion), Vorli (W orli), Mazagao (Mazgao), Thana, Bandra, Mahim, and Caranja (Uran). In 1536, Nuno da Cunha appointed his brother-in-law Garcia de Sá as the first Captain/Governor of Baçaim. The first corner stone for the Fort was laid by António Galvão. In 1548, the Governorship of Baçaim was passed on to Jorge Cabral.

Jorge Cabral

In the second half of 16th century, the Portuguese built a new fortress enclosing a whole town within the fort walls. The fort included 10 bastions, of these nine were named as: Cavalheiro, Nossa Senhora dos Remédios, Reis Magos Santiago, São Gonçalo, Madre de Deus, São João, Elefante, São Pedro, São Paulo and São Sebastião, São Sebastião was also called "Porta Pia" or pious door of Baçaim. It was through this bastion that the Marathas would enter to defeat the Portuguese. There were two medieval gateways, one on seaside called *Porta do Mar* with massive teak gates cased with iron spikes and the other one called *Porta da Terra*. There were ninety pieces of artillery, 27 of which were made of bronze and seventy mortars, 7 of these mortars were made of bronze. The port was defended by 21 gun boats each carrying 16 to 18 guns. This fort stands till today with the outer shell and ruins of churches.

In 1548, St. Francisco Xavier stopped in Baçaim, and a portion of the Baçaim population was converted to Christianity. In Salsette island, the Portuguese built 9 churches: Nirmal (1557), Remedi (1557), Sandor (1566), Agashi (1568), Nandakhal (1573), Papdi (1574), Pali (1595), Manickpur (1606), Mercês (1606). All these beautiful churches are still used by the Christian community of Vasai. In 1573 alone 1600 people were baptized.

5.7.3 17th Century

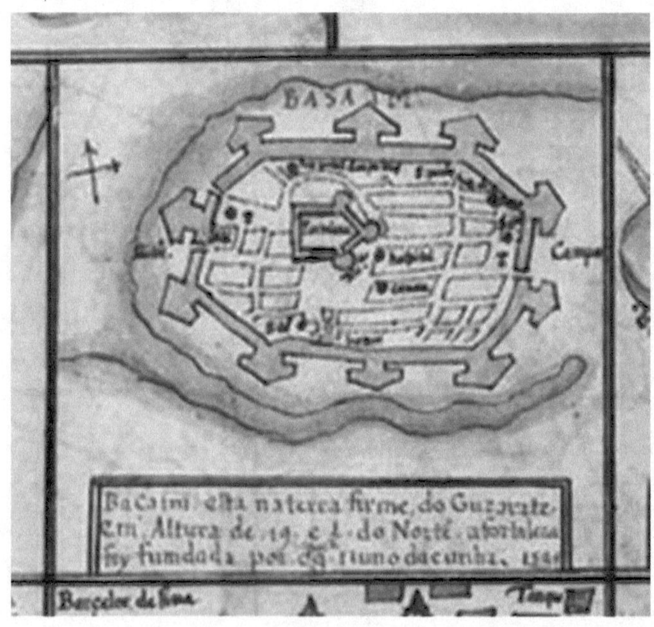

Map of Baçaim from Portuguese Atlas

As Baçaim prospered under the Portuguese, it came to be known as *"a Corte do Norte"* or "Court of the North", it became a resort to "fidalgos" or noblemen and richest merchants of Portuguese India. Baçaim became so famous that a great Portuguese man would be called *"Fidalgo ou Cavalheiro de Baçaim"* or "Nobleman of Bassein". Baçaim during the Portuguese period was known for the refinement and wealth and splendor of its buildings, palaces and for the beauty of its churches. The Bassein fort which now lies in ruins was the administrative centre and court of the northern province, and was subordinate only to Velha Goa in the south, the capital of the East Indies or the eastern faction of the Portuguese empire. The northern province consisted a territory which extended as far as 100 kilometers along the coast, in between Damaon (Daman) and Chaul (Colaba district), and in some places extended 30-50 kilometres inland. It was the most productive Indian area under Portuguese rule.

In 1618, Baçaim suffered from a succession of disasters. First it was struck by a plague then on 15 May, the city was struck by a deadly cyclone. It caused considerable damage to the boats and houses, and thousands of coconut trees were uprooted and flattened, monsoon winds had pushed brackish sea water inland. Many churches and convents of the Franciscans and Augustinians were affected by the disaster. The roofs of three of the largest churches in Bassein city including the seminary and the chapel of the Jesuits were ripped off, making the structure almost beyond repair. This storm was followed by so complete a failure of rains which resulted in famine-like conditions. In a few months, the situation grew so precarious that parents were openly selling their children to Muslim brokers into slavery rather than to starve them to death. The practice was stopped by the Jesuits, partly by saving from their own scanty allowances and partly by donations from the rich. In 1634, Baçaim's population numbered about 400 Portuguese families, 200 Indian Christian families and 1800 slaves (Indians and Africans). In 1674, Bassein had 2 colleges, 4 convents, and 6 churches.

St. James Church, Agashi

In 1674, 600 Arab pirates from Muscat landed at Baçaim. The fort garrison panicked and was too scared to oppose the pirates outside the fort walls. The pirates plundered all the churches outside of the fort walls and spared no violence and cruelty towards the people of Baçaim. In 1674, More Pundit stationed himself in Kalyan, and forced the Portuguese to pay him one-fourth of Baçaim's revenues. Two years later, Shivaji advanced near Saivan. As the Portuguese power waned towards the end of the 17th century, Baçaim suffered considerably.

The importance of Baçaim was reduced by transfer of neighboring Bombaim island to the British in 1665. The East India Company had been coveting the relatively safe Bombay Harbour for many years, even before their trading post was affected by the Sack of Surat. *Bombaim* was finally acquired by them through the royal dowry of Catherine Braganza, before that they had ventured to seize it by force in 1626 and had urged the directors of the East India Company to purchase it in 1652. The intolerance of the Portuguese to other religions seriously hindered the growth of Baçaim or Bombaim as a prosperous settlement. Their colonization efforts were not successful because they had gradually divided the lands into estates or fiefs, which were granted as rewards to deserving individuals or to religious orders on a system known as *aforamento* whereby the grantees were bound to furnish military aid to the king of Portugal or where military service was not deemed necessary, to pay a certain rent. The efficiency of the Portuguese administration was weakened by frequent transfers of officers, and by the practice of allowing the great nobles to remain at court and administer their provinces. They soon became a corrupt and opulent society based upon slave labour. The cruelties of the Inquisition (from 1560) alienated the native population of New Christians, and the Iberian Union of Portugal with Spain (1580) deprived the Indian settlements of care of the home government. The Portuguese trade monopoly with Europe could henceforth last only so long as no European rival came upon the scene.

5.7.4 18th century Maratha conquest

In 1720, one of the ports of the Northern Province, Kalyan, was conquered by the Marathas and in 1737, they took possession of Thana including all the forts in Salsette island and the forts of Parsica, Trangipara, Saibana (Present-day Saivan, south bank of the Tansa river), Ilha das Vaccas (Island of Arnala), Manora (Manor), Sabajo (Sambayo/Shabaz near Belapur), the hills of Santa Cruz and Santa Maria.

The only places in the Northern Province that now remained with the Portuguese were Chaul (Revdanda), Caranja, Bandra, Versova, Baçaim, Mahim, Quelme (Kelve/Mahim), Sirgão (Present day Shirgao), Dahanu Sao Gens (Sanjan), Asserim (Asheri/Asherigad), Tarapor (Tarapur) and Damão. By 1736, the Portuguese had been at work for 4 years constructing the fortress of Thana, and aside from the long delays, the workers were unpaid and unfed.

The locals who were tired of the oppression, finally invited the Marathas to take possession of the island of Salsette, preferring their rule to the oppression of the Portuguese. These were some of the factors that weakened Baçaim and set the stage for Maratha attacks.

After the war of 1737- 39, Chimaji appa and his Maratha soldiers took the church bells from Vasai as memorabilia and installed them in various Hindu mandirs of Maharashtra, some of the bells they installed in Khandoba mandir, Tulja bhavani mandir of Jejuri and Osmanabad respectively . These church bells are still present in these mandirs.

5.7.5 Siege of Baçaim

The siege of Baçaim began on 17 February 1739. All the Portuguese outposts around the major fort at Baçaim had been taken. Their supply routes from the north and south had been blocked, and with the English manning the seas, even that route was unreliable.

Chimaji Appa arrived at Bhadrapur near Baçaim in February 1739. According to a Portuguese account, his forces numbered 40,000 infantry, 25,000 cavalry, and around 4,000 soldiers trained in laying mines. Furthermore, he had 5,000 camels and 50 elephants.

More joined from Salsette in the following days, increasing the total Maratha troops amassed to take Baçaim to close to 100,000. The Portuguese, alarmed at this threat, decided to vacate Bandra, Versova and Dongri so as to better defend Baçaim. As per orders of the Portuguese Governor, only Baçaim, Damão, Diu and Karanja (Uran) were to be defended. These were duly fortified. In March 1739, Manaji Angre attacked Uran and captured it from the Portuguese.

This was followed by easy Maratha victories at Bandra, Versova and Dharavi which the Portuguese garrison had vacated. Manaji Angre joined Chimaji Appa at Vasai after this. Thus by April 1739, the noose around Baçaim had further tightened.

Malhar Rao Holkar I

The capture of Thana and Dharavi meant that even small boats could not reach Baçaim without being fired upon by Maratha cannons. Still, General Martinho De Silva wanted to fight a losing battle. Chimaji Appa now decided to bring down the fort of Baçaim itself. All except Vasai in Maratha hands, including the forts at Bandra, Versova, Dongri and Uran. The fort at Baçaim is situated on land with the Arabian sea on one side, and the Vasai creek on another two sides.

A painting of Chimaji Ballal Peshwa near Parvati temple in Pune

The village of Baçaim itself and the large Maratha camp at Bhadrapur were to the north. Within the fort itself, the towers of São Sebastião and Remedios faced the Marathas at Bhadrapur. The barracks and everything else was inside, with the main gate facing the Vasai creek. Chimaji Appa began the siege on 1 May 1739 by laying 10 mines next to the walls near the tower of Remedios. Maratha soldiers charged into the breach caused by exploding four of them. Almost immediately, they came under fire from Portuguese guns and muskets. Chimaji Appa, Malhar Rao Holkar, Ranoji Shinde and Manaji Angre goaded their contingents to scale the walls throughout the day. Next day on 2 May, the tower of São Sebastião and Remedios were repeatedly attacked. More mines were set off during the day, causing large breaches in the walls, between the two towers. Around 4,000 Maratha soldiers tried to pour into the fort, but the Portuguese opposition was fierce. They also managed to defend the two towers by lighting firewood. On 3 May, the tower of São Sebastião was demolished by a Maratha mine. Maratha armies could now easily march into the fort, without the fear of being fired upon from the tower. The encirclement and defeat of the Portuguese was complete. Chimaji Appa decided to settle the war at this point by sending an envoy to the Portuguese. In his letter, he warned them that the entire garrison would be slaughtered and the fort levelled if the war continued. The Portuguese commander in charge of the fort duly surrendered on 16 May 1739. On 23 May 1739, the saffron flag flew atop Baçaim.

CHAPTER 6

Maratha invasions of Bengal

6.1 First Battle of Katwa

The First Battle of Katwa occurred between Bengal Subah and Maratha Empire in 1742. The Marathas initially attacked and captured Katwa and Hooghly in Bengal. The Nawab of Bengal Alivardi Khan, using conscripted tribal and peasant levies from Birbhum, responded with a direct attack on the Maratha camp at Katwa from the rear in nightfall and the entire Maratha army was evacuated out of Bengal on 17 September 1742, believing a much larger force had charged them. The Maratha commander Bhaskar Pandit was killed during the attack on the camp.

6.2 Second Battle of Katwa

The Second Battle of Katwa occurred between the Bengal and Maratha Empire in December 1745. After the defeats of the Marathas in the first four invasions of Bengal, the Maratha General and ruler of Nagpur, Raghuji Bhonsle again invaded the territory of Bengal. Bhonsle, with 20,000 horsemen attacked the civilians of Murshidabad and moved onwards to Katwa. However he was repeatedly ambushed by peasant guerillas and militias in Birbhum and near Durgapur, and thus his column was thinned considerably. The Marathas met Alivardi Khan's army in Katwa where the battle started. During the battle, most of the Marathas were slaughtered and the remaining Maratha soldiers under Raghuji Bhonsle retreated from Katwa. The Marathas then retreated towards Medinipur. The battle was a victory for Alivardi Khan who had once again ousted the Marathas from East Bengal. After this battle, Alivardi Khan was known in Bengal as "Maratha-khuni" which translates to "Maratha-killer" in Bengali.

6.3 Battle of Burdwan

The Battle of Burdwan occurred between the Nawab of Bengal and Maratha empire in 1747. After the dismissal of Mir Jafar by Alivardi Khan, an army was amassed to defend against the invading Maratha forces of Janoji Bhonsle at Orissa. Alivardi Khan managed to heavily repulse and defeat the Maratha's in this battle.

CHAPTER 7

Maratha conquest of North-west India

The Maratha conquest of Northwest India occurred between 1757 and 1759, when the Maratha Empire captured the northwestern parts of the Indian subcontinent (in present-day Pakistan) from the Durrani Empire. It had long-lasting effects upon the future geopolitics of the Indian subcontinent.

7.1 Background

After the death of Mughal Emperor Aurangzeb in 1707, the Maratha War of Independence ended in Maratha victory. This was followed by the phase of rapid expansion of the Maratha Empire into North India for the next 50 years under the great Peshwa Baji Rao I and his equality illustrious brother Chimanji Appa. They conquered Gujarat, the whole of Central India and Orissa, subdued Rajputana and raided into Bengal and Tiruchirapalli in Tamil Nadu, and imposed chauth upon these areas. Their ambition pushed them further northwards than Delhi into Haryana, which collided with the ambitions of Ahmad Shah Abdali, the founder of Durrani Empire. In 1757, Ahmad Shah Abdali raided Delhi and captured Punjab and Kashmir with the help of Rohilla chief Najib Khan. He installed his son Timur Shah Durrani in Multan and went back to Afghanistan.

7.2 The Campaign

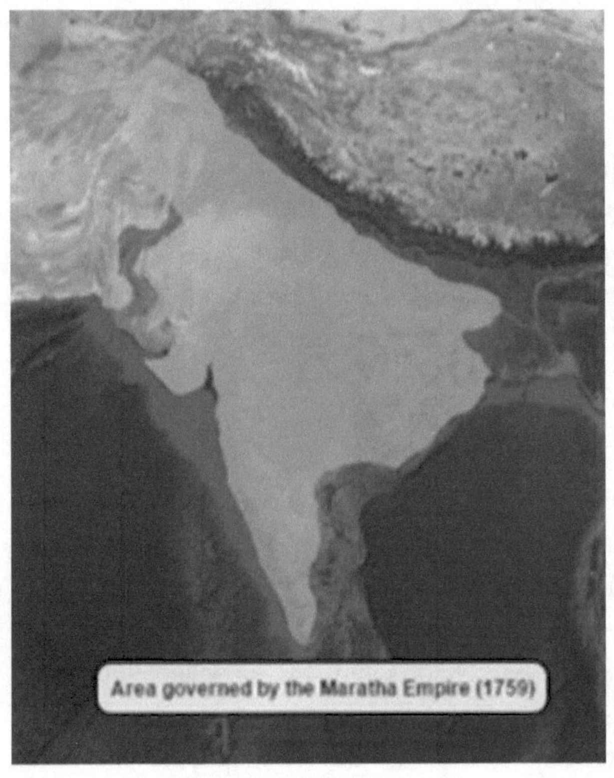

Maratha Empire circa 1758

The Maratha Peshwa Balaji Baji Rao sent his brother Raghunath Rao along with Shamsher Bahadur, Ramsingha, Gangadhar Tatya, Sakharambapu, Naroshankar, Maujiram Bania and a large army towards Delhi. They were accompanied by Malhar Rao Holkar of Malwa who had a long experience of North India and its rulers. The Marathas captured Delhi in August 1757. They decisively defeated the Rohillas and Afghans near Delhi in 1758. The defeat was so decisive that Najib Khan surrendered to the Marathas and became their prisoner.

7.2.1 Initial campaign of Sirhind

In Punjab, Adina Beg Khan, along with the Sikhs, was already in revolt with Ahmad Shah Abdali who had invaded Punjab multiple times and had been repelled each time. He decided to call the Marathas for help as a large Afghan garrison was expected to reinvade and Adina needed more alliance to battle the invaders. On 7 March, Raghunathrao had encamped at Rajpura where he received Adina Beg Khan's envoys, and was informed that the latter, accompanied by 15,000 Sikh fighters, belonging to the bands (the jathas) of Jassa Singh Ahluwalia and Baba Ala Singh of Patiala had closed upon Sirhind from the other side of Satluj. A concerted attack on the fort of Sirhind was made by the Marathas and the Sikhs on 8 March 1758. Ahmad Samad Khan, with his 10,000 Afghan troops, held out for about two weeks before his capitulation on 21 March. After the victory, the town was thoroughly sacked by the victors. After defeating the Afghan-Rohilla forces, the Marathas and Sikhs forced the Afghans into the Khyber Pass.

The Maratha and Sikh forces then gave chase to the Pathans on horseback and were in quick pursuit of them in which they went on to capture Attock and then Peshawar from the Afghans.

Maratha general Bapuji Trimbak was given the charge of guarding Multan and Dera Ghazi Khan from the Afghans.

Maratha rule in Multan was short-lived as Durrani re-captured the city in November 1759.

Adina Beg's sudden death threw Punjab into turmoil. Many of his soldiers, particularly Afghan mercenaries deserted his army camp and added to the number of freebooters, thus creating chaos and anarchy everywhere. Sikhs started again to revolt against Muslim ruling elite, which had failed to make any permanent settlement with them. Khawaja Mirza who was now the Maratha governor of Punjab could not cope with the situation. He sent an express appeal to the Peshwa for reinforcements, alerted all the junior Maratha officers to help him restore law and order in the state and he also recalled Maratha detachments from Peshawar and Attock to safeguard his position in Lahore. Tukoji Holkar and Narsoji Pandit, the Maratha commanders of Peshawar and Attock had to withdraw their troops from the frontier posts. Sabaji Scindia was now given the charge of Peshawar.

Raghunathrao and his deputy Malhar Rao were not interested in holding the position in the north for long. On their request, Peshwa had to find their substitutes. He gave supreme command of Delhi to Dattaji Scindia, while Jankoji Scindia was appointed his deputy. They proceeded towards Delhi separately at different times.

A massive army of Marathas under their new commanders, Scindias reached Machhiwara in March 1759. Like Raghunathrao, Dattaji also didn't want to stay in Punjab for long. As there was no news of Abdali's invasion, Dattaji deferred the appointment of any permanent governor in Punjab and left it to the Peshwa for decision at his convenience. After deliberations with his advisors,

Dattaji deputed Sabaji to take care of Punjab and Nwfp, Peshawar and Attock along with assistance of Bapu Rao, Dadu Rao and Sena Pandit for time being and himself left Punjab for the suppression of Najib-ud-Daula in the Ganga valley. Bapu Rao took the charge of Rohtas Fort, while other officers were appointed on the frontier posts.

Taking advantage of Sabaji's absence from Peshawar post, the Afghans marched to Peshawar. The Peshawar fort was taken by Afghans with heavy losses to the besieged Maratha garrison. Thereafter the Afghan invaders, under Jahan Khan overran Attock and threatened the Rohtas Fort. By that time, Sabaji Scindia reached the place in the Battle of Lahore, (1759) with fresh troops and a large number of Sikh fighters, who had once again allied with the Marathas. The combined forces of the Marathas and Sikhs defeated the Afghan garrison in which Jahan Khan lost his son and was himself wounded. The Afghans quickly vacated the forts of Peshawar and Attock and retreated west to Afghanistan. So, Peshawar once again fell to Marathas.

7.3 Aftermath

7.3.1 Decline of Maratha power in North-West

It was unbearable for Abdali to overlook this defeat. The Rohilla chief Najib Khan invited Abdali to avenge his defeat. He, along with his commander Jahan Khan invaded Punjab for the fifth time with a massive force of 60,000 accompanied by heavy field-guns. Trimbak Rao, the Maratha governor of Multan, with his 6000 Maratha army, made a hasty retreat towards Lahore; Sabaji Patel also vacated Peshawar without a fight and was joined by Tukoji Holkar at Attock, fleeing towards Lahore. The remaining Marathas retreated straight to Delhi from their northernmost posts at Sonipat. Unlike Marathas, who made an ignominious exist from the Punjab, the Sikhs did not allow Abdali to take on Lahore without a fight where thousands of the Sikh fighters assembled on the west Bank of Ravi to block the Afghans and fought a pitched battle against them, in which as many as 2000 Afghans were killed, fighting against the Sikhs, and the commander Jahan Khan was wounded. On 24 December 1759, a battle was fought between Dattaji and Abdali in which Dattaji's general Bhoite was defeated with a loss of 2500 Maratha soldiers after the Mughal contingent fled from the Maratha side. As a consequence of victory, Abdali managed to join forces with Najib-ud-Daula.

Najib's general Qutub Shah defeated and a Rohilla sniper killed Dattaji at Burrari Ghat near Delhi in January 1760. Abdali followed him. Peshwa Balaji Baji Rao sent his cousin Sadashivrao Bhau to repel Abdali which ultimately resulted in the Third Battle of Panipat where although Abdali won a Pyrrhic victory the material situation did not change on ground. Before going back to Afghanistan, Abdali sued for peace with Marathas blaming Najib and others for his entry in India and pointedly stating that he did not want any rivalry with the Marathas. Abdali re-instated Marathas as the "Protector of the Mughal Empire". Panipat war was a setback to the Maratha Empire in the North-west. After the Panipat war Maratha engaged with war with Sultan of Mysore Hyder Ali and Tipu Sultan both were defeated. Maratha also engaged with war with Nawab of Hyderabad and defeated Nawab of Hyderabad. Marathas also fought war with East India Company in 1785 and defeated East India Company. There was also a crisis in Maratha Leadership after sudden deaths of two successive Peshwa's.

Within 10 years, Marathas were firmly in grasp of power in the north west under the leadership of Mahadji Shinde famously leading Capture of Delhi (1771).

7.3.2 Reasons for Decline

The Marathas had failed to befriend the important party of Punjab, particularly Sikhs, even though they had not entered Punjab, they had got close enough to be aided by Sikh troops in numerous battles. They couldn't make any formal treaty with Sikhs, who along with Adina Beg had assisted them in their conquest of north-west. According to an assessment, the Sikhs were ever ready to co-operate with the Marathas, but it goes to the discredit of the Marathas that they could not make a proper confederacy with Sikhs due to their minor stature as a confederacy. Sikhs regency was highly fluid until the Marathas arrived winning for them Sirhind and Lahore. Kirpal Singh writes:

Maratha engaged war with Sultan of Mysore Hyder Ali and Tipu Sultan both were defeated. Maratha also engaged with war with Nawab of Hyderabad and defeated Nawab of Hyderabad. Maratha also fought war with East India Company in 1785 and defeated East India Company. They were also fighting against Portuguese near Thane and Surat, moreover their capital was Poona (now Pune) which was too far from Delhi to conduct immediate actions and war play. In short Marathas didn't have peaceful time in their life they always have to face battles after battles in various parts of country didn't get enough time to establish stable administration in regions which they had conquered in northwest India and Pakistan .They even decided to extend their rule up to Kandahar but several Hindu kings feared that emergence of Maratha empire can hurt their territorial interests so they invited abdali to invade India along with Muslim rulers.

Unlike Ahmad Shah Abdali who subsequently raised a cry of jihad, the Marathas couldn't mobilize their resources and make a common cause with the Sikhs in order to pay the Afghan Emperor in his own coin.

Finding the Maratha leadership completely off guard against their political foes, many Afghans who were earlier taken captives by Marathas quickly changed their loyalty towards Adina Beg and were recruited in his army. However, later on, they betrayed him and joined Abdali's forces during his fifth invasion.

The Peshwa was alarmed by the growing French and British influence in the Deccan. When Abdali invaded Punjab for the fifth time, the Marathas didn't try hard enough to save the frontier posts and instead started planning to save Delhi from another invasion.

7.4 Battle of Delhi (1757)

The Battle of Delhi in 1757 also referred to as the Second Battle of Delhi, was a battle fought on 11 August 1757 between the Maratha Empire under the command of Raghunath Rao and the Rohillas under the command of Najib-ud-Daula, who was under the Afghan suzerainty and simultaneously the "Pay Master" of what remained of the Mughal Army. The battle was waged by the Marathas for the control of Delhi, the former Mughal capital which was now under the control of Rohilla chief Najib-ud-Daula, as a consequence of the fourth invasion of India by Ahmad Shah Abdali.

7.4.1 Background

Ahmad Shah Durrani invaded North India for the fourth time in early 1757. He entered Delhi in January 1757 and kept the Mughal emperor under arrest. On his return in April 1757, Abdali re-installed the Mughal emperor Alamgir II on Delhi throne as a titular head. However, the actual control of Delhi was given to Najib-ud-Daula, who had promised to pay an annual tribute of 20 lakh rupees to Abdali. Najib had also assisted Abdali in his fourth invasion and had already won the trust of the Afghan emperor. It can be said that he worked as the agent of Abdali in Delhi court. So, Najib was now the de facto ruler of Delhi with Alamgir II as a puppet emperor in his control.

The Mughal emperor and his wazir Imad-ul-Mulk were alarmed by all these developments and hence requested Marathas to help them get rid of Abdali's agents in Delhi.

A contingent of 40,000 Maratha troops was dispatched for attacking Delhi.

7.4.2 Battle

The Marathas encamped opposite the Red Fort on the other side of Yamuna river. Najib gave the charge of 2,500 strong infantry to Qutub Shah and Mulla Aman Khan and himself commanded another infantry contingent of 5,000 troops and heavy artillery and which were deployed by him to prevent Marathas from entering the city. The battle started on 11 August and after two weeks of intense fighting, Najib surrendered and was arrested by Marathas. This power of Delhi was at last transferred from the Muslims to the Hindus.

Maratha commander Raghunath Rao demanded immediate withdrawal of Najib from Delhi along with a tribute of 50 lakh rupees. He also promised that he would never return to Delhi and never threaten any Maratha fort.

7.4.3 Aftermath

The Marathas had now become the de facto rulers of Delhi. Raghunath Rao appointed Antaji Mankeshwar as Governor of Delhi province while Alamgir II was retained as titular head with no actual power. This conquest of Delhi by the Marathas laid the foundation of their north-west campaign, as a consequence of which they established their rule up to Khyber Pass by May 1758.

7.5 Third Battle of Panipat

The Third Battle of Panipat took place on 14 January 1761 between the Maratha Empire and the invading army of the Durrani Afghan Empire. The battle took place in and around the city of Panipat, approximately 97 kilometres (60 mi) north of Delhi. The Afghans were supported by four key allies in India: the Pashtun Rohillas under the command of Najib ad-Dawlah, the Baloch Khanate of Kalat, and the Oudh State under Shuja-ud-Daula as well as elements of the declining Mughal Empire. The Maratha army was led by Sadashivrao Bhau, who was third-highest authority of the Maratha Empire after the *Chhatrapati* and the *Peshwa*. The bulk of the Maratha army was stationed in the Deccan Plateau with the *Peshwa*.

c. 1770 Faizabad-style painting of the Third Battle of Panipat; the centre of the image is dominated by the twin arcs of the lines of guns firing at each other with smoke and destruction in between.

Militarily, the battle pitted the artillery, musketry and cavalry of the Marathas against the heavy cavalry, musketry (*jezail*) and mounted artillery (*zamburak*) of the Afghans and Rohillas led by Abdali and Najib ad-Dawlah. The battle is considered to be one of the largest and most eventful fought in the 18th century, and it has perhaps the largest number of fatalities in a single day reported in a classic formation battle between two armies.

The specific site of the battle itself is disputed by historians, but most consider it to have occurred somewhere near modern-day Kaalaa Aamb and Sanauli Road. The battle lasted for several days and involved over 125,000 troops; protracted skirmishes occurred, with losses and gains on both sides. The Afghan army ultimately emerged victorious from the battle after successfully destroying several Maratha flanks. The extent of the losses on both sides is heavily disputed by historians, but it is believed that between 60,000–70,000 troops were killed in the fighting, while the numbers of injured and prisoners taken vary considerably. According to the single-best eyewitness chronicle—the *bakhar* by Shuja-ud-Daula's *Diwan Kashi Raja*—about 40,000 Maratha prisoners were collectively slaughtered on the day after the battle.

British historian Grant Duff includes an interview of a survivor of these massacres in his *History of the Marathas* and generally corroborates this number. Shejwalkar, whose monograph *Panipat 1761* is often regarded as the single-best secondary source on the battle, says that "not less than 100,000 Marathas (soldiers and non-combatants) perished during and after the battle".

7.5.1 Background

7.5.1.1 Decline of the Mughal Empire

The 27-year Mughal-Maratha war (1680–1707) led to rapid territorial loss of the Maratha Empire to the Mughal Emperor Aurangzeb. However after his death in 1707, this process reversed following the Mughal succession war between the sons of Aurangzeb. By 1712, Marathas quickly started retaking their lost lands. Under Peshwa Baji Rao, Gujarat, Malwa and Rajputana came under Maratha control. Finally, in 1737, Baji Rao defeated the Mughals on the outskirts of Delhi and brought much of the former Mughal territories in the south of Agra under Maratha control. Baji Rao's son Balaji Baji Rao further increased the territory under Maratha control by invading Punjab in 1758.

Extent of the Maratha Empire, 1760

Raghunathrao's letter to the Peshwa, 4 May 1758.

Lahore, Multan and other subahs on eastern side of Attock are under our rule for the most part, and places which have not come under our rule we shall soon bring under us. Ahmad Shah

Durrani's son Timur Shah Durrani and Jahan Khan have been pursued by our troops, and their troops completely looted. Both of them have now reached Peshawar with a few broken troops... So Ahmad Shah Durrani has returned to Kandahar with some 12–14 thousand broken troops.. Thus all have risen against Ahmad who has lost control over the region. We have decided to extend our rule up to Kandahar.

This brought the Marathas into direct confrontation with the Durrani empire of Ahmad Shah Abdali (also known as Ahmad Shah Durrani). In 1759, he raised an army from the Pashtun and Baloch tribes and made several gains against the smaller Maratha garrisons in Punjab. He then joined his Indian allies—the Rohilla Afghans of the Gangetic Doab—forming a broad coalition against the Marathas.

To counter this, Raghunathrao was supposed to go north to handle the situation. Raghunathrao asked for large number of an army soldiers, which was denied by Sadashivrao Bhau, his cousin and Diwan of Peshwa. Therefore, he declined to go. Sadashivrao Bhau was instead made commander in chief of the Maratha Army, under whom the Battle of Panipat was fought.

The Marathas, under the command of Sadashivrao Bhau, responded by gathering an army of between 45,000–60,000, which was accompanied by roughly 200,000 non-combatants, a number of whom were pilgrims desirous of making pilgrimages to Hindu holy sites in northern India. The Marathas started their northward journey from Patdur on 14 March 1760. Both sides tried to get the Nawab of Awadh, Shuja-ud-Daulah, into their camp. By late July Shuja-ud-Daulah made the decision to join the Afghan-Rohilla coalition, preferring to join what was perceived as the "army of Islam". This was strategically a major loss for the Marathas, since Shuja provided much-needed finances for the long Afghan stay in North India.

It is doubtful whether the Afghan-Rohilla coalition would have the means to continue their conflict with the Marathas without Shuja's support.

7.5.1.2 Rise of the Marathas

Sadashivrav Bhau

Grant Duff, describing the Maratha army:

The lofty and spacious tents, lined with silks and broadcloths, were surmounted by large gilded ornaments, conspicuous at a distance... Vast numbers of elephants, flags of all descriptions, the finest horses, magnificently caparisoned ... seemed to be collected from every quarter ... it was an imitation of the more becoming and tasteful array of the Mughuls in the zenith of their glory.

Engraving of a Maratha soldier by James Forbes.

The Marathas had gained control of a considerable part of India in the intervening period (1712–1757). In 1758 they nominally occupied Delhi, captured Lahore and drove out Timur

Shah Durrani, the son and viceroy of the Afghan ruler, Ahmad Shah Abdali. This was the high-water mark of Maratha expansion, where the boundaries of their empire extended north of the Sindhu river all the way down south to northern Kerala. This territory was ruled through the Peshwa, who talked of placing his son Vishwasrao on the Mughal throne. However, Delhi still remained under the control of Mughals, key Muslim intellectuals including Shah Waliullah and other Muslim clergies in India were frightened at these developments.

In desperation they appealed to Ahmad Shah Abdali, the ruler of Afghanistan, to halt the threat.

7.5.2 Prelude

Ahmad Shah Durrani (*Ahmad Shah Abdali*), angered by the news from his son and his allies, was unwilling to allow the Marathas' spread go unchecked. By the end of 1759 Abdali with his Afghan tribes, his Baloch allies, and his Rohilla ally Najib Khan had reached Lahore as well as Delhi and defeated the smaller enemy garrisons. Ahmed Shah, at this point, withdrew his army to Anupshahr, on the frontier of the Rohilla country, where he successfully convinced the Nawab of Oudh Shuja-ud-Daula to join his alliance against the Marathas. The Marathas had earlier helped Safdarjung (father of Shuja) in defeating Rohillas in Farrukhabad.

The Marathas under Sadashivrao Bhau responded to the news of the Afghans' return to North India by raising an army, and they marched North. Bhau's force was bolstered by some Maratha forces under Holkar, Scindia, Gaikwad and Govind Pant

Bundele. Suraj Mal (the Jat ruler of Bharatpur) also had joined Bhausaheb initially.

Portrait of Ahmad Shah Durrani

This combined army captured the Mughal capital, Delhi, from an Afghan garrison in December 1759. Delhi had been reduced to ashes many times due to previous invasions, and in addition there being acute shortage of supplies in the Maratha camp. Bhau ordered the sacking of the already depopulated city. He is said to have planned to place his nephew and the Peshwa's son, Vishwasrao, on the Delhi throne. The Jats withdrew their support from the Marathas. Their withdrawal from the ensuing battle was to play a crucial role in its result. Abdali drew first blood by attacking a small Maratha army led by Dattaji Shinde at Burari Ghat. Dattaji was killed in the battle.

7.5.3 Skirmishes before the battle

7.5.3.1 Afghan defeat at Kunjpura

With both sides poised for battle, maneuvering followed, with skirmishes between the two armies fought around Karnal and Kunjpura. Abdus Samad Khan, the faujdar of Sirhind, had come to Kunjpura, on the banks of the Yamuna river 60 miles to the north of Delhi with a force of more than ten thousand and supplies for the Afghan force. Kunjpura was stormed by the Marathas who was running short of supplies. Aided by the musketeers under Ibrahim Gardi, the Marathas achieved a rather easy victory at Kunjpura against an army of around 15,000 Afghans posted there. Some of Abdali's best generals like Najabat Khan were killed. Ahmad Shah was encamped on the left bank of the Yamuna River, which was swollen by rains, and was powerless to aid the garrison. The whole Afghan garrison was killed or enslaved. The massacre of the Kunjpura garrison, within sight of the Durrani camp, exasperated Abdali to such an extent that he ordered crossing of the river at all costs.

7.5.3.2 Afghans cross Yamuna

Ahmed Shah and his allies on 17 October 1760, broke up from Shahdara, marching south. Taking a calculated risk, Abdali plunged into the river, followed by his bodyguards and troops Between 23 and 25 October they were able to cross at Baghpat(a small town about 24 miles up the river), unopposed by the

Marathas who were still preoccupied with the sacking of Kunjpura and visit to nearby Kurukshetra; an important Hindu pilgrimage destination.

After the Marathas failed to prevent Abdali's forces from crossing the Yamuna River, they set up defensive works in the ground near Panipat, thereby blocking his access back to Afghanistan, just as Abdali's forces blocked theirs to the south. However, on the afternoon of 26 October, Ahmad Shah's advance guard reached Sambalka, about halfway between Sonepat and Panipat, where they encountered the vanguard of the Marathas. A fierce skirmish ensued, in which the Afghans lost 1000 men but drove the Marathas back to their main body, which kept retreating slowly for several days. This led to the partial encirclement of the Maratha army. In skirmishes that followed, Govind Pant Bundele, with 10,000 light cavalry who weren't formally trained soldiers, was on a foraging mission with about 500 men. They were surprised by an Afghan force near Meerut, and in the ensuing fight, Bundele was killed. This was followed by the loss of a contingent of 2,000 Maratha soldiers who had left Delhi to deliver money and rations to Panipat. This completed the encirclement, as Ahmad Shah had cut off the Maratha army's supply lines.

With supplies and stores dwindling, tensions started rising in the Maratha camp. Initially the Marathas had moved in almost 150 pieces of modern long-range, French-made artillery. With a range of several kilometres, these guns were some of the best of the time. The Marathas' plan was to lure the Afghan army to confront them while they had close artillery support.

7.5.3.3 Preliminary moves

During the next two months of the siege, constant skirmishes and duels took place between units from the two sides. In one of these Najib lost 3,000 of his Rohillas and was nearly killed himself. Facing a potential stalemate, Abdali decided to seek terms, which Bhau was willing to consider. However, Najib Khan delayed any chance of an agreement with an appeal on religious grounds and sowed doubt about whether the Marathas would honour any agreement.

After the Marathas moved from Kunjpura to Panipat, Diler Khan Marwat, with his father Alam Khan Marwat and a force of 2500 Pashtuns, attacked and took control of Kunjpura, where there was a Maratha garrison of 700–800 soldiers. At that time Atai Khan Baluch, son of the Shah Wali Khan, the Wazir of Abdali, came from Afghanistan with 10,000 cavalry and cut off the supplies to the Marathas.

The Marathas at Panipat were surrounded by Abdali in the south, Pashtun Tribes (Yousuf Zai, Afridi, Khattak) in the east, Shuja, Atai Khan and others in the north and other Pashtun tribes (Gandapur, Marwat, Durranis and Kakars) in the west. Unable to continue without supplies or wait for reinforcements from Pune any longer, Bhau decided to break the siege. His plan was to pulverise the enemy formations with cannon fire and not to employ his cavalry until the Afghans were thoroughly softened up. With the Afghans broken, he would move camp in a defensive formation towards Delhi, where they were assured supplies.

7.5.3.4 Formations

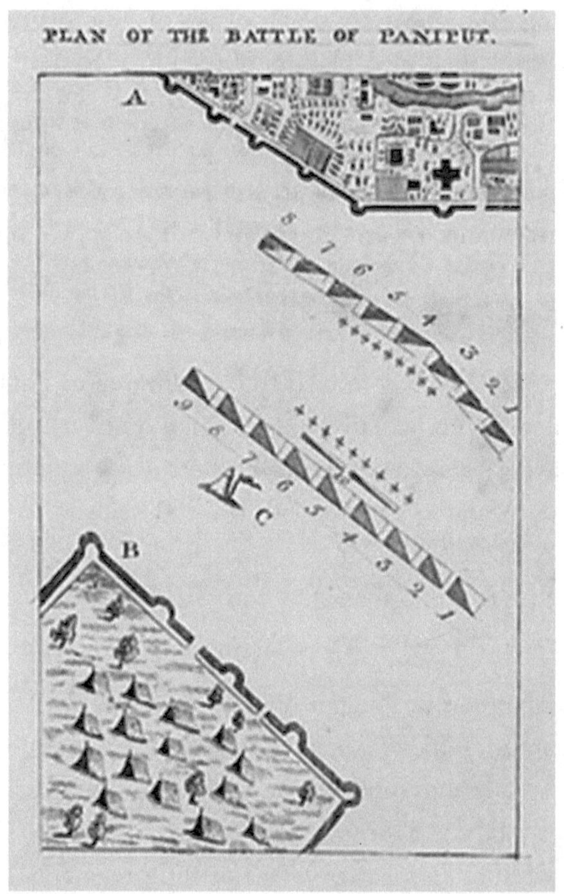

Plan of the Third Battle of Panipat based on Kashi raja (Casi Raja) Pandit's account

With the Maratha chiefs pressurizing Sadashivrao Bhau, to go to battle rather than perish by starvation, on 13 January, the Marathas left their camp before dawn and marched south towards the Afghan camp in a desperate attempt to break the siege. The two armies came face-to-face around 8:00 a.m.

The Maratha lines began a little to the north of Kala Amb. They had thus blocked the northward path of Abdali's troops and at the same time were blocked from heading south—in the direction of Delhi, where they could get badly needed supplies—by those same troops. Bhau, with the Peshwa's son and the royal guard (Huzurat), was in the centre. The left wing consisted of the *Gardis* under Ibrahim Khan. Holkar and Sindhia were on the extreme right.

The Maratha line was formed up some 12 km across, with the artillery in front, protected by infantry, pikemen, musketeers and bowmen. The cavalry was instructed to wait behind the artillery and bayonet-wielding musketeers, ready to be thrown in when control of the battlefield had been fully established. Behind this line was another ring of 30,000 young Maratha soldiers who were not battle-tested, and then the civilians. Many were ordinary men, women and children on their pilgrimage to Hindu holy places and shrines. Behind the civilians was yet another protective infantry line, of young, inexperienced soldiers.

On the other side the Afghans formed a somewhat similar line, a few metres to the south of today's Sanauli Road. Their left was being formed by Najib and their right by two brigades of troops. Their left centre was led by two Viziers, Shuja-ud-daulah with 3,000 soldiers and 50–60 cannons and Ahmad Shah's Vizier Shah Wali with a choice body of 19,000 mailed Afghan horsemen.[24] The right centre consisted of 15,000 Rohillas under Hafiz Rahmat and other chiefs of the Rohilla Pathans. Pasand Khan covered the left wing with 5,000 cavalry, Barkurdar Khan and Amir Beg covered the right with 3,000 Rohilla cavalry. Long-range musketeers were also present during the battle. In this order the army of Ahmed Shah moved forward, leaving him at his preferred post in the centre, which was now in the rear of the line, from where he could watch and direct the battle.

7.5.4 Battle

7.5.4.1 Early phases

Before dawn on 14 January 1761, the Maratha troops broke their fast with sugared water in the camp and prepared for combat. They emerged from the trenches, pushing the artillery into position on their prearranged lines, some 2 km from the Afghans. Seeing that the battle was on, Ahmad Shah positioned his 60 smooth-bore cannon and opened fire.

The initial attack was led by the Maratha left flank under Ibrahim Khan, who advanced his infantry in formation against the Rohillas and Shah Pasand Khan. The first salvos from the Maratha artillery went over the Afghans' heads and did very little damage. Nevertheless, the first Afghan attack by Najib Khan's Rohillas was broken by Maratha bowmen and pikemen, along with a unit of the famed Gardi musketeers stationed close to the artillery positions. The second and subsequent salvos were fired at point-blank range into the Afghan ranks. The resulting carnage sent the Rohillas reeling back to their lines, leaving the battlefield in the hands of Ibrahim for the next three hours, during which the 8,000 Gardi musketeers killed about 12,000 Rohillas.

In the second phase, Bhau himself led the charge against the left-of-center Afghan forces, under the Afghan Vizier Shah Wali Khan. The sheer force of the attack nearly broke the Afghan lines, and the Afghan soldiers started to desert their positions in the confusion. Desperately trying to rally his forces, Shah Wali appealed to Shuja ud Daulah for assistance. However, the Nawab did not break from his position, effectively splitting the Afghan force's center. Despite Bhau's success and the ferocity of the charge, the attack did not attain complete success as many of the half-starved Maratha mounts were exhausted. Also, there were no heavy armoured cavalry units for the Marathas to maintain these openings. In order to turn about the deserting Afghan troopers, Abdali deployed his Nascibchi musketeers to gun down the deserters who finally stopped and returned to the field.

7.5.4.2 Final phase

The Marathas, under Scindia, attacked Najib. Najib successfully fought a defensive action, however, keeping Scindia's forces at bay. By noon it looked as though Bhau would clinch victory for the Marathas once again. The Afghan left flank still held its own, but the centre was cut in two and the right was almost destroyed. Ahmad Shah had watched the fortunes of the battle from his tent, guarded by the still unbroken forces on his left. He sent his bodyguards to call up his 15,000 reserve troops from his camp and arranged them as a column in front of his cavalry of musketeers (Qizilbash) and 2,000 swivel-mounted *shutarnaals* or Ushtranaal—cannons—on the backs of camels.

The shutarnaals, because of their positioning on camels, could fire an extensive salvo over the heads of their own infantry, at the Maratha cavalry. The Maratha cavalry was unable to withstand the muskets and camel-mounted swivel cannons of the Afghans. They could be fired without the rider having to dismount and were especially effective against fast-moving cavalry. Abdali therefore, sent 500 of his own bodyguards with orders to raise all able-bodied men out of camp and send them to the front. He sent 1,500 more to punish the front-line troops who attempted to flee the battle and kill without mercy any soldier who would not return to the fight. These extra troops, along with 4,000 of his reserve troops, went to support the broken ranks of the Rohillas on the right. The remainder of the reserve, 10,000 strong, were sent to the aid of Shah Wali, still labouring unequally against the Bhau in the centre of the field. These mailed warriors were to charge with the Vizier in close order and at full gallop. Whenever they charged the enemy in front, the chief of the staff and Najib were directed to fall upon either flank.

With their own men in the firing line, the Maratha artillery could not respond to the shathurnals and the cavalry charge. Some 7,000 Maratha cavalry and infantry were killed before the hand-to-hand fighting began at around 14:00 hrs. By 16:00 hrs, the tired Maratha infantry began to succumb to the onslaught of attacks from fresh Afghan reserves, protected by armoured leather jackets.

7.5.4.3 Outflanked

Sadashiv Rao Bhau who had not kept any reserves, seeing his forward lines dwindling, civilians behind and upon seeing Vishwasrao disappear in the midst of the fighting, felt he had no choice but to come down from his elephant and lead the battle.

Taking advantage of this, the Afghan soldiers who had been captured by the Marathas earlier during the Siege of Kunjpura revolted. The prisoners unwrapped their green belts and wore them as turbans to impersonate the troops of the Durrani Empire and began attacking from within. This brought confusion and great consternation to the Maratha soldiers, who thought that the enemy had attacked from the rear. Some Maratha troops in the vanguard, seeing that their general had disappeared from his elephant and the chaos ensuing in the rear, panicked and scattered in disarray towards the rear.

Abdali had given a part of his army the task of surrounding and killing the Gardis, who were at the leftmost part of the Maratha army. Bhausaheb had ordered Vitthal Vinchurkar (with 1500 cavalry) and Damaji Gaikwad (with 2500 cavalry) to protect the Gardis. However, after seeing the Gardis having no clearing for directing their cannon fire at the enemy troops, they lost their patience and decided to fight the Rohillas themselves. Thus, they broke their position and went all out on the Rohillas. The Rohilla riflemen started accurately firing at the Maratha cavalry, which was equipped only with swords. This gave the Rohillas the opportunity to encircle the Gardis and outflank the Maratha centre while Shah Wali pressed on attacking the front. Thus the Gardis were left defenseless and started falling one by one.

Vishwasrao had already been killed by a shot to the head. Bhau and the Huzurati royal forces fought till the end, the Maratha leader having three horses shot out from under him. At this stage, the Holkar and Scindia contingents, realising the battle was lost, merged their forces with one contingent breaking from the Maratha right flank and escaped from the opening in the Durrani lines southwards as Jankoji Rao Scindia lead the other contingent to reinforce the thinning lines of Marathas.[1] The Maratha front lines remained largely intact, with some of their artillery units fighting until sunset. Choosing not to launch a night attack, many Maratha troops escaped that night. Bhau's wife Parvatibai, who was assisting in the administration of the Maratha camp, escaped to Pune with her bodyguard, Janu

Bhintada along with Nana Fadnavis under the protection of Malhar Rao Holkar's contingent. Some 15,000 soldiers managed to reach Gwalior.

7.5.5 Reasons for the outcome

Durrani had both numeric as well as qualitative superiority over Marathas. The combined Afghan army was much larger than that of Marathas. Though the infantry of Marathas was organized along European lines and their army had some of the best French-made guns of the time, their artillery was static and lacked mobility against the fast-moving Afghan forces. The heavy mounted artillery of Afghans proved much better in the battlefield than the light artillery of Marathas. None of the other Hindu Kings joined forces to fight Abdali. Allies of Abdali, namely, Najib, Shuja and the Rohillas knew North India very well. He was also diplomatic, striking agreements with Hindu leaders, especially the Jats and Rajputs, and former rivals like the Nawab of Awadh, appealing to him in the name of religion.

Moreover, the senior Maratha chiefs constantly bickered with one another. Each had ambitions of carving out their independent states and had no interest in fighting against a common enemy. Some of them did not support the idea of a *pitched battle* and wanted to fight using guerrilla tactics instead of charging the enemy head-on. The Marathas were fighting alone at a place which was 1000 miles away from their capital Pune.

Raghunathrao was supposed to go north to reinforce the army. Raghunathrao asked for large amount of wealth and troops, which was denied by Sadashivrao Bhau, his cousin and Diwan of Peshwa, so he declined to go. Sadashivrao Bhau was there upon made commander in chief of the Maratha Army, under whom the Battle of Panipat was fought. Some historians have opined, that Peshwa's decision to appoint Sadashivrao Bhau as the Supreme Commander instead of Malharrao Holkar or Raghunathrao proved to be an unfortunate one, as Sadashivrao was totally ignorant of the political and military situation in North India.

If Holkar had remained in the battlefield, the Maratha defeat would have been delayed but not averted. Ahmad Shah's superiority in pitched battle could have been negated if the Marathas had conducted their traditional ganimi kava, or guerrilla warfare, as advised by Malharrao Holkar, in Punjab and in north India. Abdali was in no position to maintain his field army in India indefinitely.

7.5.6 Massacres after the battle

The Afghan cavalry and pikemen ran wild through the streets of Panipat, killing tens of thousands of Maratha soldiers and civilians. Afghan officers who had lost their kin in battle were permitted to carry out massacres of Marathas the next day also, in Panipat and the surrounding area. They arranged victory mounds of severed heads outside their camps. According to the single best eyewitness chronicle – the bakhar by Shuja-ud-Daula's Diwan Casi Raja(Kashi Raja) – about 40,000 Maratha prisoners were slaughtered in cold blood the day after the battle.[12][13] According to Hamilton, a reporter of the Bombay Gazette, about half a million Marathi people were present there in Panipat town and he gives a figure of 40,000 prisoners as executed by Afghans. Some 22,000 women and children were driven off as slaves.

All of the prisoners were transported on bullock carts, camels and elephants in bamboo cages.

Siyar-ut-Mutakhirin says:

The unhappy prisoners were paraded in long lines, given a little parched grain and a drink of water, and beheaded... and the women and children who survived were driven off as slaves — twenty-two thousand, many of them of the highest rank in the land.

7.5.7 Aftermath

Mahadaji Shinde restored Maratha domination over northern India, within a decade after the war.

The bodies of Vishwasrao and Bhau were recovered by the Marathas and were cremated according to their custom. Bhau's wife Parvatibai was saved by Holkar, per the directions of Bhau, and eventually returned to Pune.

Peshwa Balaji Baji Rao, uninformed about the state of his army, was crossing the Narmada with a relief force and supplies when he heard of the defeat. He returned to Pune and never recovered from the shock of the debacle at Panipat. According to Kashi Raja Pundit, "It was Balaji Bajirao's love of pleasure which was responsible for Panipat. He delayed at Paithan celebrating his second marriage until December 27, when it was too late."

Jankoji Scindia was taken prisoner and executed at the instigation of Najib. Ibrahim Khan Gardi was tortured and executed by enraged Afghan soldiers. The Marathas never fully recovered from the loss at Panipat, but they remained the largest empire in the Indian subcontinent and managed to retake Delhi ten years later. However, their claim over all of India ended with the three Anglo-Maratha Wars, in the early 19th century.

The Jats under Suraj Mal benefited significantly from not participating in the Battle of Panipat. They provided considerable assistance to the Maratha soldiers and civilians who escaped the fighting.

Though Abdali won the battle, he also had heavy casualties on his side and sought peace with the Marathas. Abdali sent a letter to Nanasaheb Peshwa (who was moving towards Delhi, albeit at a very slow pace to join Bhau against Abdali) appealing to the Peshwa that he was not the one who attacked Bhau and was just defending himself. Abdali wrote in his letter to Peshwa on 10 February 1761:

There is no reason to have animosity amongst us. Your son Vishwasrao and your brother Sadashivrao died in battle, was unfortunate. Bhau started the battle, so I had to fight back unwillingly. Yet I feel sorry for his death. Please continue your guardianship of Delhi as before, to that I have no opposition. Only let Punjab until Sutlaj remain with us. Reinstate Shah Alam on Delhi's throne as you did before and let there be peace and friendship between us, this is my ardent desire. Grant me that desire.

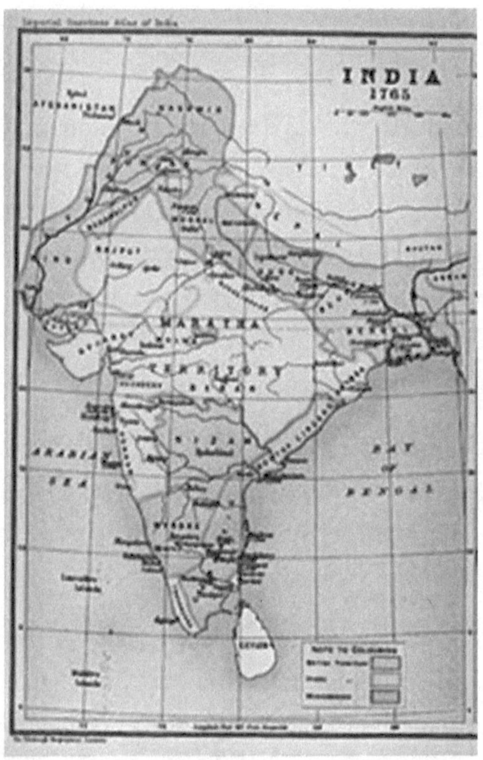

Map of India in 1765, before the fall of Nawabs and Princely states nominally allied to the emperor (mainly in Green).

These circumstances made Abdali leave India at the earliest. Before departing, he ordered the Indian chiefs, through a Royal Firman (order) (including Clive of India), to recognise Shah Alam II as Emperor.

Ahmad Shah also appointed Najib-ud-Daula as ostensible regent to the Mughal Emperor. In addition, Najib and Munir-ud-daulah agreed to pay to Abdali, on behalf of the Mughal king, an annual tribute of four million rupees. This was to be Ahmad Shah's final major expedition to North India, as the losses in the battle left him without the capacity to wage any further war against the Marathas, and as he became increasingly preoccupied with the rise of the Sikhs.

Shah Shuja's forces (including Persian advisers) played a decisive role in collecting intelligence against the Maratha forces and was notorious in ambushing the leading in hundreds of casualties.

After the Battle of Panipat the services of the Rohillas were rewarded by grants of Shikohabad to Nawab Faiz-ullah Khan and of Jalesar and Firozabad to Nawab Sadullah Khan. Najib Khan proved to be an effective ruler. However, after his death in 1770, the Rohillas were defeated by the forces of the British East India Company. Najib died on 30 October 1770.

To save their kingdom, the Mughals once again changed sides and welcomed the Afghans to Delhi. The Mughals remained in nominal control over small areas of India but were never a force again. The empire officially ended in 1857 when its last emperor, Bahadur Shah II, was accused of being involved in the Indian Rebellion and exiled.

The result of the battle was the temporary halting of further Maratha advances in the north and destabilisation of their territories for roughly ten years. This period is marked by the rule of Peshwa Madhavrao, who is credited with the revival of Maratha domination following the defeat at Panipat. In 1771, ten years after Panipat, Mahadji Shinde led a large Maratha army into northern India in a punitive expedition which re-established Maratha domination in that area and punished refractory powers that had either sided with the Afghans, such as the Rohillas, or had shaken off Maratha domination after Panipat. But their success was short-lived. Crippled by Madhavrao's untimely death at the age of 28, infighting ensued among Maratha chiefs soon after, and they were ultimately defeated and annexed by the British East India Company administration in 1818.

7.5.8 Legacy

The valour displayed by the Marathas was extolled by Ahmad Shah Abdali in his letter to his ally, Madho Singh, the king of Jaipur.

The Marathas fought with the greatest valour which was beyond the capacity of other races... These dauntless blood-shedders did not fall short in fighting and doing glorious deeds.... Suddenly the breeze of victory began to blow... and the wretched Deccanis suffered defeat.

The battle was referred to in Rudyard Kipling's poem "With Scindia to Delhi".

Our hands and scarfs were saffron-dyed for signal of despair,

When we went forth to Paniput to battle with the ~Mlech~,

Ere we came back from Paniput and left a kingdom there.

It is, however, also remembered as a scene of valour on both sides. Atai Khan, the adopted son of the Wazir Shah Wali Khan, was said to have been killed during this time when Yeshwantrao Pawar climbed atop his elephant and struck him down. Santaji Wagh's corpse was found with over 40 mortal wounds.

CHAPTER 8

Maratha Resurrection

The Maratha Resurrection was the period between the Third Battle of Panipat on January 14, 1761 and capture of Najibabad in 1772.

In the Third Battle of Panipat, the Maratha Empire suffered a serious blow at the hands of the Muslim alliance of the Durrani Empire, Mughal Empire, under Prince Ali Gohar later known as (Shah Alam II) (r. 1760 – 1806)and his Nawab of Awadh, and Rohillas under Najib ad-Dawlah. Their power was virtually wiped out of northern India and the confederacy itself experienced fragmentation. The Bhonsles of Nagpur did not participate and tried to remain aloof of the aftermath as well.

After the death of Peshwa Balaji Baji Rao Bhat, Madhavrao I became Peshwa under the regency of Raghunathrao Bhat. Despite quarrels with Raghunathrao, the young Peshwa, along with Mahadji Shinde and Nana Fadnavis, were able to resurrect Maratha supremacy, both in Deccan and Delhi.

Madhavrao Peshwa's victory over the Nizam of Hyderabad and Hyder Ali of Mysore in southern India proved Maratha dominance in the Deccan.

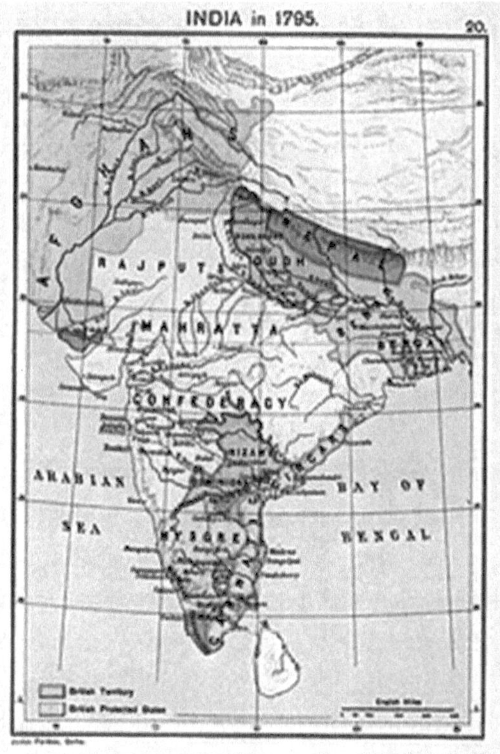

Maratha Confederacy in year 1795.

On the other hand, Mahadji's victory over Jats of Mathura, Rajputs of Rajasthan and Pashtun-Rohillas of Rohilkhand (in the western part of present-day Uttar Pradesh state) re-established the Marathas in the northern India.

With the Capture of Delhi in 1771 and the capture of Najibabad in 1772 and treatise with Mughal Emperor Shah Alam II as a restricted monarch to the throne under Maratha suzerainty, the resurrection of Maratha power in the North was complete.

8.1 Restoration of Maratha suzerainty in the North

Under Madhavrao Peshwa, Maratha authority in North India (including Delhi) was restored ten years after the battle of Panipat. The Rohillas were defeated and were forced to pay a heavy war indemnity. Delhi was captured by Mahadji Scindia in late 1770 and restored Mughal emperor Shah Alam II to the throne of Delhi in 1772.

8.2 Battle of Alegaon

The Battle of Alegaon was fought between Nizam Ali Khan of Hyderabad and Raghunathrao of the Maratha Empire against Madhavrao I of the Maratha Empire. Raghunathrao had established an alliance with Nizam Ali Khan of Hyderabad. When conflict arose between Raghunathrao and Madhavrao I, a joint campaign between Nizam Ali Khan and Raghunathrao resulted in Madhavrao I being heavily defeated. Madhavrao I surrendered on 12 November 1762. Nizam Ali Khan got all of his previously lost territories that were lost at the Battle of Udgir. Madhavrao I submitted to his uncle, Raghunathrao.

8.3 Battle of Rakshasbhuvan

The Battle of Rakshasbhuvan in India was fought on 10 August 1763. After the defeat of the Marathas at the Battle of Panipat, their rivals started seizing the opportunity to recover their losses in the past at the hands of Marathas. Particularly, the Nizam of Hyderabad wanted to recover territory he had lost at the Battle of Udgir where all of his dukes and earls were killed. He decided to launch a war on the Marathas.

8.3.1 Battle

To boost the morale of his army, on the advice of his Diwan Vithal Sundar Pratapwant, the son of Sundar Narayan, who had renovated the Kala Ram temple at Nasik (Historian Ninad Bedekar mentions Vithal Sundars surname as "Parshurami") he declared Inams and Jagirs to many warriors who had deserted the Marathas and had joined with him to replace his warriors who were killed at Udgir. The main warrior amongst them was Vinayak Dasrao, nephew of Vithal Sundar himself, the other lieutenants being Narsinha Dixit Kaygaonkar whose father was killed in one of battle in Bundelkhand fighting for Marathas, Shankarji Joshi and Krishnarao Kanitkar.

The latter 3 were given Jagirs of Kaygaon Toke, Badnapur and Limbaganesh whilst Vinayak Dasrao was given Inam of Neuregaon. Vithal Sundar was given Jagir of the most fertile area of Pimpri in Aurangabad District. Amongst these, Krishnarao Kanitkar had given refuge to Vyankatrao Ghorpade of Ichalkaranji, Sardar Kolhatkar of Pen (Brother-in-law of Sadashivrao Peshwa) and Sardar Hariba Patwardhan of Sangli during their flight from Scindia's forces during the mutiny of the pretender of Sadashiv Bhau. This refuge was given at the request of Sardar Tukoji Holkar.

Over and above the army of 25,000 of these Jagirdars from the Marathi area and loyal forces of Ismail Khan Panni, Raghoji Jadhavrao IV and Nanasaheb Nimbalkar Khardekar, Nizam was also assisted by General Bussey's French troops. However, the Marathas were being led by Peshwa Madhavrao (until the skirmish of Chambhar Gonda, Senasahebsubha Janoji Bhonsle and Raghunathrao, uncle of Peshwa were also in the camp), who was assisted by Visaji Tryambak, Sardar Naro Shankar Dani, Babuji Naik (A Chief of Senasahebsubha's Nagpur Army who, prior to battle a few months before, had made a friendship treaty with Nizam), Sardar Yashwantrao/Santajirao Wable (Kopergaon) and Sardar Malojiraje III Ghorpade of Mudhol trounced the Nizam's forces at Rakshasbhuvan after the battle was fought for five to six months. Many of Nizam's trusted dukes like Shambhulal, Hamid Ulla Khan, Laxmanrao Khandagale, Rukn Ud Doula, Ramchandrarao Jadhavrao of Bhalki, Mir Moghal Ali Khan alias Nasir Ul Mulk left Nizam after the throne was encroached by Nizam Ali, brother of dethroned Nizam Salabat Jung and joined Marathas.

Ironically Govindrao Ghorpade, who fought on behalf of the Nizam, was killed at the hands of his father, Malojirao Ghorpade, who was with Marathas. The Nizam's closest aide, Vithal Sundar, was killed by Sardar Mahadaji Shitole Deshmukh of Kasba Pune.

8.3.2 Truce

A truce was reached and a treaty was signed at Aurangabad, whereby the Nizam lost 50 lacs territory including Bhalki and except Telangana and the eastern part of the Godavari river in Maharashtra. They gained the Bidar and Naldurg forts in exchange for Bhalki.

As a part of the settlement, Neurgaon and Limbaganesh became part of the Maratha empire. After the defeat of Marathas in 1818, the British returned this territory to Nizam IV and these two Jagirs got merged into Nizam State. This led to Salar Jung II advising 5th Nizam to terminate their Jagirs.

As a result, the Jagirs of Neurgaon, Badnapur and Kaygaon got merged with the Jagir of Takli/Lad Sawangi. Troops of Limbaganesh got merged with 5000 Mansab of Aamir Nawaz Khan, Talukdar of Naldurg and Collector of Bhir in 1843 which were restored by Sir Sikandar Khan's father during his reign in 1888.

This decisive victory made Marathas stronger. Surprisingly Vithal Sundar's vacant post of Diwan was given to Mir Musa Khan Rukn Ud Daula, a Peshwa lobbyist in Nizam's durbar.

8.4 Capture of Delhi (1771)

The Capture of Delhi was a battle in 1771 when the forces of the Maratha Empire led by Mahadaji Shinde captured Delhi along with the Red Fort, and giving Mughal Emperor Shah Alam II the throne back with treaty. The Marathas captured Delhi from the Afghans under Najib Khan. With this battle Marathas regained their lost supremacy in North India after the Third Battle of Panipat and conquered much of the lost territories which they lost after the Third Battle of Panipat.

In the Third Battle of Panipat, the Maratha Empire suffered a serious blow at the hands of the Muslim axis of the Durrani Empire, Nawab of Awadh, and Rohillas under Najib ad-Dawlah. After the death of Peshwa Balaji Baji Rao Bhat, Madhavrao I became Peshwa under the regency of Raghunathrao Bhat. Mahadaji's victory over Jats of Mathura, Rajputs of Rajasthan and Pashtun-Rohillas of Rohilkhand (in the western part of present-day Uttar Pradesh state) re-established the Marathas in the northern India.

8.4.1 Aftermath

After taking control of Delhi, Marathas sent a large army in 1772 to "punish" Afghan Rohillas for Panipat. Maratha army devastated Rohilkhand by looting and plundering and also took the members of royal family as captives. Maratha general Mahadaji was "very much pleased with the revenge taken by his men" for Panipat. Najib Khan's son and Nawab of Rohilkhand Zabita Khan was defeated by the Marathas, led by Mahadaji Sindhia (shinde) in 1772 and the fort of Pathargarh (Najibabad) was completely looted by the Marathas in the form of horses, elephants, guns and other valuable things, to avenge the deaths of Maratha warriors who fell in the battle of Delhi and Panipat. Marathas also destroyed grave of Najib, scattering his bones all around.

CHAPTER 9

Maratha–Mysore Wars

The Maratha–Mysore Wars was a conflict in the 18th century India, between the Maratha Empire and the Kingdom of Mysore. Though initial hostilities between the sides started in 1770s, the last warfare began on February 1785 and ended in 1787.

9.1 Situation in the 18th century

18th century saw a steady decline of once a dominant power on the whole subcontinent – Mughal Empire. Apart from the disastrous invasion by the Afsharid ruler of Iran, Nader Shah in 1739, Mughals were successfully contested by Maratha Empire. Meanwhile, the British East India Company was asserting its influence in India and was engaged in a series of wars with Mysore which eventually resulted in the region falling under Company rule.

9.1.1 Mysore wars with the British

Mysore was a relatively small kingdom in the beginning of 1700s. However, able rulers such as Hyder Ali and Tipu

Sultan transformed the kingdom and westernized the army that it soon turned into a military threat both to the British and Maratha Empire. Upon Haidar Ali's death, Mysore covered 80,000 sq. miles and had a population of approximately 6 million.

Starting from 1767, Kingdom of Mysore had overall had four major military confrontations (1767–69; 1780–84; 1790–92; and 1799).

About 1761, commander in chief of the state of Mysore, Hyder Ali proclaimed himself absolute ruler of the Kingdom and started military campaigns to expand the territory of the state. In 1766, the British East India Company joined forces with the local ruler of Hyderabad against Hyder Ali, but by 1769, the British were left alone in a war with Mysore Kingdom. In 1769 Hyder Ali made his way to Madras (location of the Company's government) and demanded a peace treaty.

9.1.2 Maratha-Mysore Wars

Although clashes between the Mysore ruler Hyder Ali and Marathas had taken place occasionally before 1785, the actual warfare started in February 1785.

After the Second Anglo-Mysore War, the ruler of Mysore Tipu Sultan sought to keep offensive moves by the Marathas at bay. Marathas had established a military alliance with the ruler of Hyderabad with a common purpose of recovering territories both had lost to Mysore in previous conflicts. Much of the desired territory was subject to marches, countermarches, and sieges of fortified points. The Marathas also attempted to draw the British East India Company into the pending conflict, but a neutrality policy implemented by the new governor-general, Lord Charles Cornwallis made its participation impossible.

9.1.3 Major conflicts

- Battle of Rutehalli Fort (1764)
- Battle of Sira and Madgiri (1767)
- Battle of Chinkurli (1771)
- Battle of Saunshi (1777)
- Siege of Nargund, February 1785
- Siege of Badami, May 1786
- Siege of Adoni, June 1786
- Battle of Gajendragad, June 1786
- Battle of Savanur, 10 October 1786
- Siege of Bahadur Benda, January 1787

9.1.4 Outcome

The Maratha-Mysore War ended after the final conflict during the siege of Bahadur Benda in January 1787, and later settled for peace with the kingdom of Mysore, to which Tipu Sultan obliged with the signing of the treaty of Gajendragad in April 1787. Tipu had to pay an annual tribute of 12 lakhs per year to the Marathas, thus ending hostilities with them, which allowed him to focus on his rivalry with the British. The Battle of Gajendragadh was fought between the Marathas and Tipu Sultan from March 1786 to March 1787 in which Tipu Sultan was defeated by the Marathas. By the victory in this battle, the border of the Maratha territory extended till Tungabhadra river.

Maratha-Mysore war ended in April 1787, following the finalizing of *treaty of Gajendragad*, as per which, Tipu Sultan of Mysore was obligated to pay 4.8 million rupees as a war cost to the Marathas, and an annual tribute of 1.2 million rupees. In addition to returning all the territory captured by Hyder Ali, Tipu also agreed to pay 4 year's arrears of the tribute, which Mysore owed to the Marathas, through Hyder Ali.

Tipu would release Kalopant and return Adoni, Kittur, and Nargund to their previous rulers. Badami would be ceded to the Marathas. Tipu would also pay an annual tribute of 12 lakhs per year to the Marathas. In return, Tipu would get all the places that they had captured in the war, including Gajendragarh and Dharwar. Tipu would also be addressed by the Marathas by an honorary title of "Nabob Tipu Sultan, Fateh Ali Khan". In Fourth Anglo-Mysore War maratha empire presented its support to the East India Company.

9.2 Battle of Rutehalli Fort

In 1764, following the attack by Hyder Ali on Nawabs of Savanur, who were a tributary to the Marathas, Maratha army led by Peshwa Madhav Rao met the forces of Hyder Ali at Rutehalli Fort. Hydar Ali tried to avoid pitched battles against Maratha Forces however Maratha forces intercepted Mysore forces near Rutehalli Fort in Karnatic and a crushing defeat was imposed upon them, Hydar Ali lost well over 1,000 men and himself fled into the local forest to save his life.

9.3 Battle of Sira and Madgiri

In 1767, Maratha army led by Peshwa Madhav Rao defeated the forces of Hyder Ali at Sira and Madgiri. Marathas conquered the forts of Haskote and Nandigarh and laid siege to Bednur where Hyder Ali was taking shelter.

9.4 Battle of Saunshi

The Battle of Saunshi was fought between the Sultanate of Mysore and the Maratha Empire in 1777. Hyder Ali attempted to try to regain his lost territories of Malabar and Coorg from the Marathas and was successful in doing so. Hyder Ali decided to attack the Marathas at Saunshi. Hyder Ali sent his trusted general Muhammad Ali to attack the Maratha garrison stationed at Saunshi. The result of the battle was a decisive victory for Mysore and Hyder Ali against the Maratha forces. Maratha Chief Konher Rao was killed in the battle and Padurang Rao was captured and taken as a prisoner by the Mysore forces.

9.5 Siege of Nargund

The Siege of Nargund occurred when the Kingdom of Mysore sent its General, Burhanuddin to besiege Nargund. In 1778, Tipu Sultan defeated the Marathas and captured Nargund. Tipu decided to keep its Brahmin ruler, Vyankatrao Bhave, as long as he recognizes Tipu Sultan's supremacy and paid an annual tribute.

The Brahmin ruler later become non-compliant and sought help with the Maratha ruler, Nana. Nana supported Bhave with 5,000 troops. Burhanuddin laid siege to Nargund and on July 29, 1785, Nargund once again was conquered by the Kingdom of Mysore after Vyankatrao Bhave and Kalopant Pethe surrendered.

9.5 Siege of Adoni

The Siege of Adoni occurred between the forces of Tipu Sultan of the Kingdom of Mysore and the Maratha Empire allied with the Nizam of Hyderabad. Tipu Sultan surprised Haripant when he decided to advance for Adoni. In 1786, Adoni was besieged for one month and then captured by Tipu Sultan.

9.6 Battle of Savanur

The Battle of Savanur concluded in October, 1786, with the victory of Tipu Sultan over the Marathas. Tipu strategically lured the Marathas out of their position on a height near Savanur and unleashed a barrage of heavy fire on them. This devastated the Maratha army, making them retreat and Tipu Sultan conquered Savanur soon after.

9.7 Siege of Bahadur Benda

The Siege of Bahadur Benda happened between the forces of Tipu Sultan of Mysore and the Maratha forces of Haripant. Tipu Sultan defeated the Maratha forces. Following this battle, a peace agreement was signed between the Empire of Mysore and the Maratha Empire, which allowed for Tipu Sultan to focus his resources into combating the British Empire.

9.8 Battle of Gajendragad

The Battle of Gajendragad was fought in June 1786, during the Maratha-Mysore War. An army of the Maratha Empire led by Tukoji Rao Holkar, defeated the army of Tipu Sultan and captured the town and fortress at Gajendragad. Mysore was obligated to pay 4.8 million rupees as a war cost to the Marathas, and an annual tribute of 1.2 million rupees. The *treaty of Gajendragad* signed after the battle ended the Maratha-Mysore conflict.

CHAPTER 10

First Anglo-Maratha War

The First Anglo-Maratha War (1775–1782) was the first of three Anglo-Maratha Wars fought between the British East India Company and Maratha Empire in India. The war began with the Treaty of Surat and ended with the Treaty of Salbai. The war was fought in between Surat and Pune Kingdom saw British defeat and restoration of positions of both the parties before the war. Warren Hastings, the first President and Governor-General of East India Company's provinces in India decided not to attack Poona directly.

10.1 Background

After the death of Madhavrao Peshwa in 1772, his brother Narayanrao became peshwa (prime minister) of the Maratha Empire. Narayanrao was murdered by his palace guards in August 1773, and his uncle Raghunathrao (Raghoba) became Peshwa. However, Narayanrao's wife, Gangabai, gave birth to a posthumous son, who was the legal heir to the throne. The newborn infant was named 'Sawai' Madhavrao (*Sawai* means "One and a Quarter"). Twelve Maratha chiefs, known as the Baarbhai and led by Nana Phadnavis, directed an effort to install the infant as the new Peshwa and to rule in his name as regents.

Raghunathrao, unwilling to give up his position of power, sought help from the British at Bombay and signed the Treaty of Surat on 6 March 1775. According to the treaty, Raghunathrao ceded the territories of Salsette and Bassein (Vasai) to the British, along with part of the revenues from Surat and Bharuch districts. In return, the British promised to provide Raghunathrao with 2,500 soldiers.

The British Calcutta Council condemned the Treaty of Surat, sending Colonel Upton to Pune to annul it and make a new treaty with the regency. The Treaty of Purandhar (1 March 1776) annulled that of Surat, Raghunathrao was pensioned and his cause abandoned, but the revenues of Salsette and Broach districts were retained by the British. The Bombay government rejected this new treaty and gave refuge to Raghunathrao. In 1777, Nana Phadnavis violated his treaty with the Calcutta Council by granting the French a port on the West coast. The English retaliated by sending a force towards Pune.

10.2 Initial stage and Treaty of Purandar (1775–1776)

British troops under the command of Colonel Keating, left Surat on March 15, 1775, for Pune. But they were checked by Haripant Phadke at Adas and were totally defeated on May 18, 1775. Casualties for Keating's force, accompanied by Raghunathrao, included 96 killed. The Marathas casualties in the Battle of Adas (Gujarat) included 150 killed.

Warren Hastings estimated that direct actions against Pune would be detrimental. Therefore, the Supreme Council of Bengal condemned the Treaty of Surat, sending Colonel Upton to Pune to annul it and make a new treaty with the regency. An agreement between Upton and the ministers of Pune called Treaty of Purandar was signed on March 1, 1776.

The Treaty of Purandhar (1 March 1776) annulled that of Surat, Raghunath Rao was pensioned and his cause abandoned, but the revenues of Salsette and Broach districts were retained by the British.

10.3 Battle of Wadgaon

The Battle of Wadgaon (12–13 January 1779) was a battle fought between the Maratha Empire and the British East India Company near Vadgaon Maval village in Maharashtra and was part of the First Anglo-Maratha War.

10.3.1 Background

The port of Bombay (Mumbai) had been under British rule since 1661. Towards the second half of the 18th century, with the rise of the Maratha Empire, the British felt the need to secure the port and taking control of the supply routes to it from Bassein (now known as Vasai) to the north and from Pune to the east, both of which were part of the Maratha Empire. Also, the Marathas had started negotiations with the French, which was alarming for the British.

With this objective, on 6 March 1775 the British entered into the Treaty of Surat with Raghunathrao who was a claimant to the Peshwa throne. As per the treaty, Raghunathrao would be installed as Peshwa and in return would cede Salsette and Bassein Fort to the British.

10.3.2 British in the Bor Ghat

The campaign began in November 1778, when British forces under Capt. James Stewart and Col. Egerton, among others proceeded from Mumbai towards Pune via the Bor Ghat (this ghat was also used by Shivaji on his return from Surat and currently is part of Mumbai – Pune railway). Col. Egerton captured the Belapur fort and established a base at Panvel, while Capt. Stewart proceeded to Khandala (22nd November 1778). The British forces number nearly 4000, inclusive of artillery and gun lashkars. Small contingents of infantry and cavalry were also with Raghunath Rao. The British were counting on Nana Phadnis to resist at Pune with a force of 7-8 thousand. Moreover, the British resident at Pune, Mr. Mostyn was convinced that Shinde and Holkar would desert Pune and join Raghoba as soon as the British were in sight! Both proved to be fatal errors for the British.

From Panvel, Col. Egerton reached Khopoli and established a second British base in the valley in the winter of 1778 . Capt. James Stewart had by then reached the village of Khandala and established a camp at the top of the ghat. Col Egerton followed suit and by the middle of December, a large British force had assembled there. Col. Egerton then divided his forces between Lt. Col Cay and Lt. Col Cockburn. Throughout the march from the fort at Mumbai, they had faced no resistance from the Marathas and the morale was thus sky high in the British camp.

10.3.3 Preliminaries

The East India Company's force from Bombay consisted of about 3,900 men (about 600 Europeans, the rest Asian) accompanied by many thousands of servants and specialist workers. They were joined on the way by Raghunath Rao's forces, adding several thousand more soldiers, and more artillery.

The Maratha army included forces contributed by all the partners in the federation, tens of thousands in all, commanded by Tukojirao Holkar and General Mahadji Shinde.

Mahadji slowed down the British march and sent forces west to cut off its supply lines. When they found out about this, the British halted at Talegaon, a few hours' brisk march from Pune, but days away for the thousands of support staff with their ox-drawn carts. Now the Maratha cavalry harassed the enemy from all sides. The Marathas also utilized a scorched earth strategy, vacating villages, removing food-grain stocks, burning farmland and poisoning wells.

10.3.4 Battle

The British began to withdraw from Talegaon in the middle of the night, but the Marathas attacked, forcing them to halt in the village of Wadgaon (now called Vadgaon or Vadgaon Maval), where the British force was surrounded on 12 January 1779.

By the end of the next day, the British were ready to discuss surrender terms, and on 16 January signed the 'Treaty of Wadgaon', the terms of which forced the Bombay government to relinquish all territories acquired by the Bombay office of the East India Company since 1773, the halting of a British force marching towards Pune from Bengal; and a share of revenues from the district of Broach (Bharuch).

10.3.5 Aftermath

In a spirit of chivalry, the Marathas permitted the British to retreat to Bombay. As per British historian James Douglas, this proved to be a strategic mistake with ramifications not just for the Maratha Empire, but the history of India, when he said that had Nana Fadnavis, the powerful minister in Pune, been like Napoleon or Edward I, no British soldier would have survived to tell the tale and the whole course of history of India would have been different. The treaty of Wadgaon did not last very long and the British Governor-General in Bengal, Warren Hastings, rejected the treaty on the grounds that the Bombay officials had no legal power to sign it, and ordered that British interests be secured in the area.

Reinforcements from northern India, commanded by Colonel (later General) Thomas Wyndham Goddard, arrived too late to save the Bombay force.

Goddard with 6,000 troops stormed Bhadra Fort and captured Ahmedabad on February 15, 1779. There was a garrison of 6,000 Arab and Sindhi infantry and 2,000 horses. Losses in the fight totalled 108, including two British. Goddard also captured Bassein on December 11, 1780.

Another Bengal detachment led by Captain Popham and assisted by the Rana of Gohad, captured Gwalior on August 4, 1780, before Mahadji Scindia could make preparations. Skirmishes took place between Mahadji Scindia and General Goddard in Gujarat, but indecisively. Hastings sent yet another force to harass Mahadji Shinde, commanded by Major Camac.

10.4 Central India and the Deccan

A Vijay Stambh (Victory Pillar) erected to commemorate Maratha victory over British. The pillar is located at Vadgaon/Wadgaon Maval, close to the city of Pune, India

An information plaque describing the Maratha victory over British. The plaque is located at Vadgaon/Wadgaon Maval, close to the city of Pune, India

After capturing Bassein, Goddard marched towards Pune. But he was routed in the Battle of Bhor Ghat in April 1781 by Parshurambha, Haripant Phadke and Tukoji Holkar.

In central India, Mahadji stationed himself at Malwa to challenge Camac. Initially, Mahadji had an upper hand and British forces under Camac, being harassed and reduced, had to retreat to Hadur.

In February 1781 the British beat Shinde to the town of Sipri, but every move they made after that was shadowed by his much larger army, and their supplies were cut off, until they made a desperate night raid in late March, capturing not only supplies, but even guns and elephants. Thereafter, the military threat from Shinde's forces to the British was much reduced.

The contest was equally balanced now. Where Mahadji scored a significant victory over Camac at Sironj, the latter avenged the loss through the Battle of Durdah on March 24, 1781.

Colonel Murre arrived with fresh forces in April 1781 to assist Popham and Camac. After his defeat at Sipri, Mahadji Shinde got alarmed. Finally, he decisively crushed the forces of Murre on July 1, 1781. Mahadji seemed to be too powerful to be defeated now.

10.5 Treaty of Salbai

This treaty, known as the Treaty of Salbai, was signed on 17 May 1782, and was ratified by Hastings in June 1782 and by Nana Phadnavis in February 1783. The treaty ended the First Anglo-

Maratha War, restored the status quo, and established peace between the two parties for 20 years.

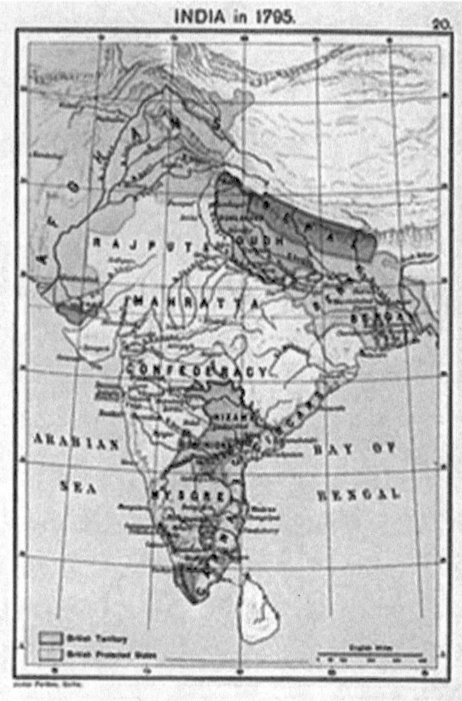

Maratha territory in year 1795 in the aftermath of the war.

10.6 Battle of Patan

The Battle of Patan was fought on 20 June 1790 between the Maratha Kingdom of Gwalior supported by Peshwa & Holkar and the alliance formed by the Rajput Kingdom of Jaipur, Kingdom of Jodhpur and Mughals under Ismail Beg which resulted in a decisive Maratha victory.

10.6.1 Stakeholders

The forces of the Rajput alliance had 12,000 Rathore cavalry, 6,000 Kachwaha cavalry, 7,000 Mughal Cavalry and 30,000 infantry with 129 Pieces of Artillery.

10.6.2 Ambush by the Marathas

At dusk, Rajputs and their allies, retired to their respective camps. The Maratha army however held its positions at the mouth of the pass. The real battle however precipitated in the evening by an unforeseen skirmish. Some Maratha Pindaris from the left wing of Maratha lines, managed to seize animals that were a part of Ismail Beg's contingent. This inevitably led to a small skirmish with Ismail Beg's men. General de Boigne then directed his guns on Ismail Beg's contingent. Caught on unaware, the murderous fire of Maratha guns proved to be deadly. Gopal Bhau and de Boigne, sensing victory, went for the kill. Marathas descended upon enemy camps. Taken aback by the suddenness and the ferocity of the Maratha attack, Rajput resistance capitulated, many were slaughtered in their sleep while others were too intoxicated to fight. The only event worth noting was the Rathor charge on the Maratha right wing. The 4,000 strong Holkar contingent was saved by swift reinforcements sent by Gopal Bhau. The Jaipur Nagas were forced in their positions by the two battalions sent by Boigne. De Boigne after routing the centre and left wing of the alliance, turned all of his forces to the right. The Rathors were soon surrounded and routed, resulting in heavy losses and the death of the Jodhpur general Gangaram. The Gwalior army did not lose any officers apart from two wounded.

The victory at Patan destroyed the armies of the two most powerful Rajput kingdoms of India and forced them to pay heavy tributes to the Peshwas and Scindias. Ismail Beg's army was also reduced to a few hundred men and were forced to flee.

10.6.3 Aftermath

Pitted against European armed and French trained Marathas, Rajput states capitulated one after the other. Marathas managed to conquer Ajmer and Malwa from Rajputs. Although Jaipur and Jodhpur remained unconquered. Battle of Patan, effectively ended Rajput hopes for independence from external interference. Sir Jadunath Sarkar notes:

From the day of Patan (20th June 1790) to the 2nd of April 1818 when Jaipur entered into protective subsidiary alliance with the British government, lay the gloomiest period in the history of Jaipur kingdom.

His victory increased Scindia's influence with the Peshwas (Maratha Prime Ministers) in Pune, the seat of Maratha government and firmly established Maratha influence in Rajputana.

10.7 Battle of Merta, 1790

The forces of Mahadji Shinde under de Boigne routed the Marwar army.

10.8 Capture of Ajmer, 1790

The forces of Mahadji Shinde captured Ajmer.

10.9 Capture of Shimoga

The Capture of Shimoga, a town and fortress held by forces of the Kingdom of Mysore, occurred on 3 January 1792, after a preliminary battle with the attacking forces of the British East India Company and the Marathas, not far from the town on 29 December, had scattered much of its defending army. The defenders surrendered after the fort's walls were breached. The battle was part of a campaign during the Third Anglo-Mysore War by Maratha leader Purseram Bhow to recover Maratha territories taken by Hyder Ali in an earlier conflict between Mysore and the Marathas. By the end of the siege, Reza Sahib a leading Mysore commander, was among the captured.

10.10 Battle of Kharda

The Battle of Kharda took place in 1795 between Nizam and Maratha Empire, in which Nizam was badly defeated. Governor General John Shore followed the policy of non-intervention despite that Nizam was under his protection. So this led to the loss of trust with the British. This was the last battle fought together by all the Maratha chiefs under leadership of Bakshibahaddar Jivabadada Kerkar. Maratha forces consisted of cavalry, including gunners, bowmen, artillery and infantry.

After several skirmishes Nizams infantry under Raymond launched an attack on the Marathas but Scindia forces under Jivabadada Kerkar defeated them and launched a counter attack which proved to be decisive. The rest of the Hyderabad army fled to the fort of Kharda. The Nizam started negotiations and they were concluded in April 1795.

Chimnaji Phatak, his son Balkrishna Phatak, Balkrishna Latey were among those who served the Peshwa's camp during the war.

10.11 Battle of Malpura

Combined force of Rathores and Kachhawaha Rajputs defeated Maratha Force under Daulat Rao Scindia.

CHAPTER 11

Second Anglo-Maratha War

The Battle of Assaye, a painting by J.C. Stadler

The Second Anglo-Maratha War (1803–1805) was the second conflict between the British East India Company and the Maratha Empire in India.

Political map of India in 1792, compared to yellow borders of 1700.

11.1 Background

The British had supported the "fugitive" Peshwa Raghunathrao in the First Anglo-Maratha War, continued with his "fugitive" son, Baji Rao II. Though not as martial in his courage as his father, the son was "a past master in deceit and intrigue". Coupled with his "cruel streak", Baji Rao II soon provoked the enmity of Yashwant Rao Holkar when he had one of Holkar's relatives killed.

The Maratha Empire at that time consisted of a confederacy of five major chiefs: the Peshwa (Prime Minister) at the capital city of Poona, the Gaekwad chief of Baroda, the Scindia chief of Gwalior, the Holkar chief of Indore, and the Bhonsale chief of Nagpur. The Maratha chiefs were engaged in internal quarrels among themselves. Lord Mornington, the Governor-General of British India had repeatedly offered a subsidiary treaty to the Peshwa and Scindia, but Nana Fadnavis refused strongly. In October 1802, the combined armies of Peshwa Baji Rao II and Scindia were defeated by Yashwantrao Holkar, ruler of Indore, at the Battle of Poona. Baji Rao fled to British protection, and in December the same year concluded the Treaty of Bassein with the British East India Company, ceding territory for the maintenance of a subsidiary force and agreeing to treaty with no other power. The treaty would become the "death knell of the Maratha Empire".

11.2 War

Battle of Assaye 1st Battalion 8th Regiment of Native Infantry charge at the cannon, led by Captain Hugh Macintosh

This act on the part of the Peshwa, their nominal overlord, horrified and disgusted the Maratha chieftains; in particular, the Scindia rulers of Gwalior and the Bhonsale rulers of Nagpur and Berar contested the agreement.

The British strategy included Wellesley securing the Deccan Plateau, Lake taking Doab and then Delhi, Powell entering Bundelkhand, Murray taking Badoch, and Harcourt neutralizing Bihar. The British had available over 53,000 men to help accomplish their goals.

In September 1803, Scindia forces lost to Lord Gerard Lake at Delhi and to Arthur Wellesley at Assaye. In November, Lake defeated another Scindia force at Laswari, followed by Wellesley's victory over Bhonsle forces at Argaon (now Adgaon) on 29 November 1803.

11.3 Conclusion

On 17 December 1803, Raghoji II Bhonsale of Nagpur signed the Treaty of Deogaon in Odisha with the British after the Battle of Laswari and gave up the province of Cuttack (which included Mughal and the coastal part of Odisha, Garjat/the princely states of Odisha, Balasore Port, parts of Midnapore district of West Bengal).

On 30 December 1803, the Daulat Scindia signed the Treaty of Surji-Anjangaon with the British after the Battle of Assaye and Battle of Argaon and ceded to the British Rohtak, Gurgaon, Ganges-Jumna Doab, the Delhi-Agra region, parts of Bundelkhand, Broach, some districts of Gujarat and the fort of Ahmmadnagar.

Yashwant Rao decided to fight against the British on his own. Yashwantrao was somewhat successful as he harassed the British forces by guerilla warfare. However, he didn't receive the expected help from Scindia who had already signed a treaty with the British. He went to Punjab and sought Ranjeet Singh's help with no success. The lack of resources compelled him to come to terms with British.

The Treaty of Rajghat, signed on 24 December 1805, forced Holkar to give up Tonk, Rampura, and Bundi.

11.4 Battle of Delhi (1803)

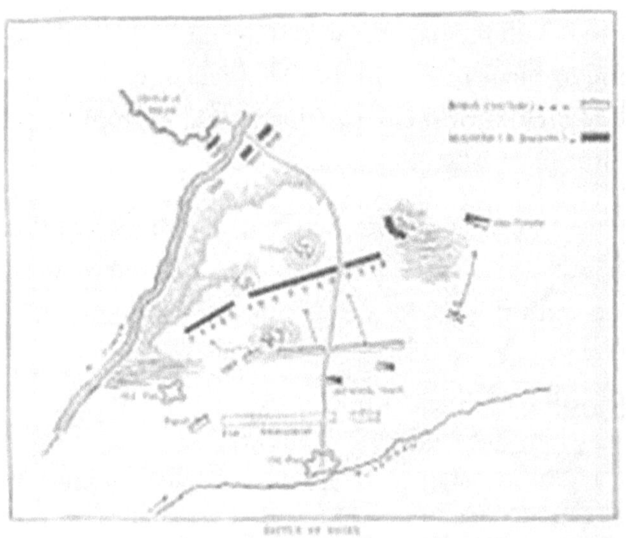

Map of the Battle of Delhi (1803)

The Battle of Delhi took place on 11 September 1803 during the Second Anglo-Maratha War, between British troops under General Lake, and Marathas of Scindia's army under General Louis Bourquin and Sardar Ravsaheb Wable.

11.4.1 Events

"Bourquin had treacherously deserted his former friend General Perron and now commanded 18 battalions of the latter's troops" The battle was fought at Patparganj, right across the Yamuna River from Humayun's Tomb, also giving the battle its local name.

The Marathas initially occupied a strong position with the Yamuna River in their rear. But, General Gerard Lake, feigning a retreat, drew them from their lines and then turning upon them drove them with the bayonet into the river, inflicting more losses upon them. Finally, the city of Delhi fell three days later. As a result, the control of the city of Delhi passed from the Marathas to the British.

A monument was later erected at the site in Patparganj, marked out by a surrounding ditch, commemorating Cornet Sanguine and British soldiers who fell during the battle.

11.5 Siege of Bharatpur (1805)

Siege of Bharatpur or Second Anglo-Maratha War took place between 2 January and 22 February 1805 in the Indian Princely state of Bharatpur (now part of Rajasthan), during the Second Anglo-Maratha War. Forces of the British East India Company, led by General Gerard Lake, were four times repulsed in attempts to storm the fortress. The victory at

Bharatpur, backed by the Maratha Empire, was an embarrassing defeat for the British.

Colonel Maitland at Bhurtpore

11.5.1 Background

The Ruler of Bharatpur, Ranjit Singh had promised to join the British but instead formed an alliance with the Ruler of Indore Yashwantrao Holkar, who was allied to the Maratha Empire. Holkar suffered setbacks with the British at the Battle of Deeg and the Siege of Deeg. However, Ranjit Singh "came out openly on Holkar's side after the defeat of Monson." Lake arrived at the Bharatpur fort on 2 January 1805.

11.5.2 Siege

The British bombardment started on 7 January, 1805, and a breach was effected on 9 January. The first British assault took place that night, led by Col. Ryan, Maj. Hawkes and Lt. Col. Maitland. The assault failed with 400 British casualties, including Maitland being mortally wounded. A second attack on 16 Jan was also thrown back, after the Marathas added water to their moat. British casualties were 500, including the assault leader, Lt. Col. MacRoy. However, Lake continued to receive supplies and reinforcements, including Maj. Gen. R. Jones force of 1600. This helped Lake deal with Amir Khan, Holkar's general, who was raiding Bundelkhand. A third assault on 20 February also failed, as did a fourth assault the next day. British casualties for all four assaults were 3,292. "The worst part of it was that many of the wounded were left behind where they had fallen. The defenders sallied out from the fort and killed them."

11.5.3 Aftermath

Ranjit Singh decided to accept the British offer, and paid the British an indemnity, which allowed him to retain all his possessions, including Deeg. Caught between three British armies, led by Lake, Gen. Jones and Col. Ball, Holkar sent emissaries to Lake. A treaty was signed on 24 December 1805, in which he gave up any claim to Tonk, Rampura, and Bundi.

CHAPTER 12

Third Anglo-Maratha War

Indian camp scene

The Third Anglo-Maratha War (1817–1819) was the final and decisive conflict between the English East India Company and the Maratha Empire in India. The war left the Company in control of most of India. It began with an invasion of Maratha territory by British East India Company troops, and although the British were outnumbered, the Maratha army was decimated. The troops were led by Governor General Hastings, supported by a force under General Thomas Hislop. Operations began against the Pindaris, a band of Muslim mercenaries and Marathas from central India.

Peshwa Baji Rao II's forces, supported by those of Mudhoji II Bhonsle of Nagpur and Malharrao Holkar III of Indore, rose against the East India Company. Pressure and diplomacy convinced the fourth major Maratha leader, Daulatrao Shinde of Gwalior, to remain neutral even though he lost control of Rajasthan.

British victories were swift, resulting in the breakup of the Maratha Empire and the loss of Maratha independence. Several minor battles were fought by the Peshwa's forces to prevent his capture.

The Peshwa was eventually captured and placed on a small estate at Bithur, near Kanpur. Most of his territory was annexed and became part of the Bombay Presidency. The Maharaja of Satara was restored as the ruler of his territory as a princely state. In 1848 this territory was also annexed by the Bombay Presidency under the doctrine of lapse policy of Lord Dalhousie. Bhonsle was defeated in the battle of Sitabuldi and Holkar in the battle of Mahidpur. The northern portion of Bhonsle's dominions in and around Nagpur, together with the Peshwa's territories in Bundelkhand, were annexed by British India as the Saugor and Nerbudda Territories. The defeat of the Bhonsle and Holkar also resulted in the acquisition of the Maratha kingdoms of Nagpur and Indore by the British. Along with Gwalior from Shinde and Jhansi from the Peshwa, all of these territories became princely states acknowledging British control. The British proficiency in Indian war-making was demonstrated through their rapid victories in Khadki, Sitabuldi, Mahidpur, and Satara.

12.1 The Marathas and the British

Map of India after the Second Anglo-Maratha War, 1805

The Maratha Empire was founded in 1674 by Shivaji of the Bhosle dynasty. Shivaji led resistance efforts to free the Hindus from the Mughals and Muslim Sultanate of Bijapur and established rule of the Hindus. This kingdom was known as the Hindavi Swarajya ("Hindu self-rule") in the Marathi language. Shivaji's capital was located at Raigad. Shivaji successfully defended his empire from attacks by the Mughal Empire and his Maratha Empire went on to defeat and overtake it as the premier power in India within few decades. A key component of the Maratha administration was the council of eight ministers, called the *Ashta Pradhan* (council of eight). The senior-most member of the Ashta Pradhan was called the *Peshwa* or the *Pant Pradhan* (prime minister).

12.1.1 Growing British power

While the Marathas were fighting the Mughals in the early 18th century, the British held small trading posts in Mumbai, Madras and Calcutta. The British fortified the naval post of Mumbai after they saw the Marathas defeat the Portuguese at neighbouring Vasai in May 1739. In an effort to keep the Marathas out of Mumbai, the British sent envoys to negotiate a treaty. The envoys were successful, and a treaty was signed on 12 July 1739 that gave the British East India Company rights to free trade in Maratha territory. In the south, the Nizam of Hyderabad had enlisted the support of the French for his war against the Marathas. In reaction to this, the Peshwa requested support from the British, but was refused. Unable to see the rising power of the British, the Peshwa set a precedent by seeking their help to solve internal Maratha conflicts. Despite the lack of support, the Marathas managed to defeat the Nizam over a period of five years.

During the period 1750–1761, British defeated the French East India Company in India, and by 1793 they were firmly established in Bengal in the east and Madras in the south. They were unable to expand to the west as the Marathas were dominant there, but they entered Surat on the west coast via the sea.

The Marathas marched beyond the Indus as their empire grew. The responsibility for managing the sprawling Maratha empire in the north was entrusted to two Maratha leaders, Shinde and Holkar, as the Peshwa was busy in the south. The two leaders did not act in concert, and their policies were influenced by personal interests and financial demands. They alienated other Hindu rulers such as the Rajputs, the Jats, and the Rohillas, and they failed to diplomatically win over other Muslim leaders. A large blow to the Marathas came in their defeat on 14 January 1761 at Panipat against a combined Muslim force that gathered defeating Marathas led by the Afghan Ahmad Shah Abdali. An entire generation of Maratha leaders lay dead on the battlefield as a result of that conflict. However, between 1761 and 1773, the Marathas regained the lost ground in the north.

12.1.2 Anglo-Maratha relations

The Maratha gains in the north were undone because of the contradictory policies of Holkar and Shinde and the internal disputes in the family of the Peshwa, which culminated in the murder of Narayanrao Peshwa in 1773. Raghunathrao was ousted from the seat of Peshwa due to continuing internal Maratha rivalries. He sought help from the British, and they signed the Treaty of Surat with him in March 1775. This treaty gave him military assistance in exchange for control of Salsette Island and Bassein Fort.

The treaty set off discussions amongst the British in India as well as in Europe because of the serious implications of a confrontation with the powerful Marathas. Another cause for concern was that the Bombay Council had exceeded its constitutional authority by signing such a treaty. The treaty was the cause of the start of the First Anglo-Maratha War. This war was virtually a stalemate, with no side being able to defeat the other. The war concluded with the treaty of Salabai in May 1782, mediated by Mahadji Shinde. The foresight of Warren Hastings was the main reason for the success of the British in the war. He had destroyed the anti-British coalition and created a division between the Shinde, the Bhonsle, and the Peshwa.

The Marathas were still in a very strong position when the new Governor General of British controlled territories Cornwallis arrived in India in 1786. After the treaty of Salabai, the British followed a policy of coexistence in the north. The British and the Marathas enjoyed more than two decades of peace, thanks to the diplomacy of Nana Phadnavis, a minister in the court of the 11-year-old Peshwa Sawai Madhavrao. The situation changed soon after Nana's death in 1800. The power struggle between Holkar and Shinde caused Holkar to attack the Peshwa in Pune in 1801, since the Peshwa sided with Shinde. The Peshwa Baji Rao II fled Pune to safety on a British warship. Baji Rao feared loss of his own powers and signed the treaty of Bassein. This made the Peshwa in effect a subsidiary ally of the British.

In response to the treaty, the Bhonsle and Shinde attacked the British, refusing to accept the betrayal of their sovereignty to the British by the Peshwa. This was the start of the Second Anglo-Maratha War in 1803. Both were defeated by the British, and all Maratha leaders lost large parts of their territory to the British.

12.1.3 Maratha-Hyderabad Relations

In 1762, Raghunathrao allied with the Nizam due to mutual distrust and differences with Madhavrao Peshwa. The Nizam marched towards Poona, but little did he know that Rughunathrao was going to betray him. In 1763, Madhavrao I along with Raghunathrao defeated Nizam at Battle of Rakshasbhuvan and signed a treaty with the Marathas. In 1795, he was defeated by Madhavrao II's Marathas at the Battle of Kharda and was forced to cede Daulatabad, Aurangabad and Sholapur and pay an indemnity of Rs. 30 million. A French general, Monsieur Raymond, served as his military leader, strategist and advisor.

The Battle of Kharda took place in 1795 between Nizam and Maratha Confederacy, in which Nizam was badly defeated. Governor General John Shore followed the policy of non-intervention despite that Nizam was under his protection. So this led to the loss of trust with the British. This was the last battle fought together by all the Maratha chiefs under leadership of Bakshibahaddar Jivabadada Kerkar. Maratha forces consisted of cavalry, including gunners, bowmen, artillery and infantry. After several skirmishes Nizams infantry under Raymond launched an attack on the Marathas but Scindia forces under Jivabadada Kerkar defeated them and launched a counter attack which proved to be decisive. The rest of the Hyderabad army fled to the fort of Kharda. The Nizam started negotiations and they were concluded in April 1795.

12.1.4 The British East India Company

The British had travelled thousands of miles to arrive in India. They studied Indian geography and mastered local languages to deal with the Indians. At the time, they were technologically advanced, with superior equipment in several critical areas to that available locally. Chhabra hypothesizes that even if the British technical superiority were discounted, they would have won the war because of the discipline and organization in their ranks. After the First Anglo-Maratha war, Warren Hastings declared in 1783 that the peace established with the Marathas was on such a firm ground that it was not going to be shaken for years to come.

The British believed that a new permanent approach was needed to establish and maintain continuous contact with the Peshwa's court in Pune. The British appointed Charles Malet, a senior merchant from Bombay, to be a permanent Resident at Pune because of his knowledge of the languages and customs of the region.

12.2 Prelude

The Maratha Empire had partly declined due to the Second Anglo-Maratha War. Efforts to modernize the armies were half-hearted and undisciplined: newer techniques were not absorbed by the soldiers, while the older methods and experience were outdated and obsolete. The Maratha Empire lacked an efficient spy system, and had weak diplomacy compared to the British. Maratha artillery was outdated, and weapons were imported. Foreign officers were responsible for the handling of the imported guns; the Marathas never used their own men in considerable numbers for the purpose. Although Maratha infantry was praised by the likes of Wellington, they were poorly led by their generals and heavily relied on Arab and Pindari mercenaries. The confederate-like structure that evolved within the empire created a lack of unity needed for the wars.

Mountstuart Elphinstone

At the time of the war, the power of the British East India Company was on the rise, whereas the Maratha Empire was on the decline. The British had been victorious in the previous Anglo-Maratha war and the Marathas were at their mercy. The Peshwa of the Maratha Empire at this time was Baji Rao II. Several Maratha leaders who had formerly sided with the Peshwa were now under British control or protection. The British had an arrangement with the Gaekwad dynasty of the Maratha province of Baroda to prevent the Peshwa from collecting revenue in that province. Gaekwad sent an envoy to the Peshwa in Pune to negotiate a dispute regarding revenue collection. The envoy, Gangadhar Shastri, was under British protection. He was murdered, and the Peshwa's minister Trimbak Dengle was suspected of the crime.

The British seized the opportunity to force Baji Rao into a treaty. The treaty (The Treaty of Pune) was signed on 13 June 1817. Key terms imposed on the Peshwa included the admission of Dengle's guilt, renouncing claims on Gaekwad, and surrender of significant swaths of territory to the British. These included his most important strongholds in the Deccan, the seaboard of Konkan, and all places north of the Narmada and south of the Tungabhadra rivers. The Peshwa was also not to communicate with any other powers in India. The British Resident Mountstuart Elphinstone also asked the Peshwa to disband his cavalry.

12.2.1 Maratha planning

Ruins of the old palace at Raigad fort

The Peshwa disbanded his cavalry, but secretly asked them to stand by, and offered them seven months' advance pay. Baji

Rao entrusted Bapu Gokhale with preparations for war. In August 1817, the forts at Sinhagad, Raigad, and Purandar were fortified by the Peshwa. Gokhale secretly recruited troops for the impending war. Many Bhils and Ramoshis were hired. Efforts were made to unify Bhonsle, Shinde, and Holkar; even the mercenary Pindaris were approached. The Peshwa identified unhappy Marathas in the service of the British Resident Elphinstone and secretly recruited them. One such person was Jaswant Rao Ghorpade. Efforts were made to secretly recruit Europeans as well, which failed. Some people, such as Balaji Pant Natu, stood steadfastly with the British. Several of the sepoys rejected the Peshwa's offers, and others reported the matter to their superior officers. On 19 October 1817, Baji Rao II celebrated the Dassera festival in Pune, where troops were assembled in large numbers. During the celebrations, a large flank of the Maratha cavalry pretended they were charging towards the British sepoys but wheeled off at the last minute. This display was intended as a slight towards Elphinstone and as a scare tactic to prompt the defection and recruitment of British sepoys to the Peshwa's side. The Peshwa made plans to kill Elphinstone, despite opposition from Gokhale. Elphinstone was fully aware of these developments thanks to the espionage work of Balaji Pant Natu and Ghorpade.

Maratha powers were estimated at 81,000 infantry, 106,000 horse or cavalry and 589 guns. Of these the Peshwa had the highest number of cavalry at 28,000, along with 14,000 infantry and 37 cannon. The Peshwa headquarters was in Pune. Holkar had the second largest cavalry, amounting to 20,000, and an infantry force supplemented with 107 artillery units. Shinde and Bhonsle had similar numbers of cavalry, artillery and infantry.

Holkar, Shinde and Bhonsle were headquartered in Indore, Gwalior and Nagpur respectively. The Afghan leader Amir Khan was located in Tonk in Rajputana and his strength was 12,000 cavalry, 10,000 infantry and 200 guns. The Pindaris were located north of the Narmada valley in Chambal and Malwa region of central India. Three Pindari leaders sided with Shinde, these were Chitu, Karim Khan and Wasil Mohammad. They led horsemen with strengths of 10,000, 6,000 and 4,000 but most were armed only with spears. The rest of the Pindari chiefs, Tulsi, Imam Baksh, Sahib Khan, Kadir Baksh, Nathu and Bapu were allied with Holkar. Tulsi and Imam Baksh each had 2,000 horsemen, Kadir Baksh, 21,500. Sahib Khan, Nathu and Bapu had 1,000, 750 and 150 horsemen.

12.2.2 British planning

The East India Company viewed the killing of their envoy, Gangadhar Shastri, as definitive intent by the Peshwa to undermine British control over the Maratha, and operations were commenced in order to place the entire region effectually into the possession of the Company. Although some regard the war as a mopping-up operation of the earlier Second Anglo-Maratha war, historians note the fact that the British assembled the largest army they had ever at that time organised in India indicated the importance the British placed on defeating the Maratha. The army, numbering roughly 120,000 men, consisted of the Grand Army or Bengal Army under the command of the Marquess of Hastings, and the Army of the Deccan under General Hislop. This included over 60 battalions of Native Infantry, multiple battalions derived from British regiments, numerous sections of cavalry and dragoons, in addition to artillery, horse artillery and rocket troops, all armed with the most modern weapons and equipped with highly organised supply lines.

This massive force quickly induced Shinde, who was secretly planning with the Peshwa and the Nepal Ministry to form a coalition against the British, into coming to terms with the British. In early November 1817, he was forced to enter into a treaty in which he ceded all his armed forces and major forts. Amir Khan disbanded his army on condition of being guaranteed the possession of the principality of Tonk in Rajputana. He sold his guns to the British and agreed to prevent predatory gangs from operating from his territory. By these actions, the British kept two major allies of the Maratha out of the war before any hostilities had begun.

12.3 Major events of the war

12.3.1 Conflict in Pune and the pursuit of Baji Rao II

The war began as a campaign against the Pindaris, but the first battle occurred at Pune where the Peshwa, Baji Rao II, attacked the under-strength British cantonment on 5 November 1817. The Maratha forces comprised 20,000 cavalry, 8,000 infantry, and 20 artillery guns whereas the British had 2,000 cavalry, 1,000 infantry, and eight artillery units. What followed was the Battle of Khadki where the Maratha were initially successful in creating and exploiting a gap in the British lines, but were soon nullified by the advance of the British infantry, which firing volley after volley, caused the Maratha to retreat in a matter of four hours. The British soon claimed victory with the loss of 86 men compared to the 500 Maratha killed.

The Marquess of Hastings

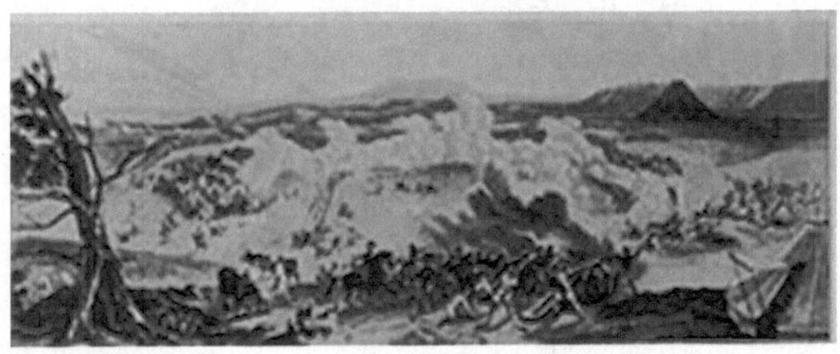

Battle of Khadki, 1817

While Pune was surrendered to the British, the Peshwa and his forces fled first to Purandar and then toward the city of Satara. His commander-in-chief Bapu Gokhale organised the retreat to guard the Peshwa in flight. The Peshwa then fled to the town of Koregaon where the Battle of Koregaon (also known as the battle of Koregaon Bhima) took place on 1 January 1818 on the banks of the river Bhima, north west of Pune. Captain Stauton arrived near Koregaon along with 500 infantry, two six-pounder guns, and 200 irregular horsemen. Only 24 of the infantry were of European origin; they were from the Madras Artillery. The rest of the infantry was composed of Indian sepoys employed by the British. A fierce battle ensued that lasted the entire day. Streets and guns were captured and recaptured, changing hands several times. Although Baji Rao's commander Trimabkji killed Lieutenant Chishom, the Marathas were forced to evacuate the village and retreated during the night. The British lost 175 men and about a third of the irregular horse, with more than half of the European officers wounded. The Marathas lost 500 to 600 men.

After the battle the British forces under general Pritzler pursued the Peshwa, who fled southwards towards Karnataka with the Raja of Satara. The Peshwa continued his flight southward throughout the month of January. Not receiving support from the Raja of Mysore, the Peshwa doubled back and passed General Pritzler to head towards Solapur. Until 29 January the pursuit of the Peshwa had not been productive. Whenever Baji Rao was pressed by the British, Gokhale and his light troops hovered around the Peshwa and fired long shots. Some skirmishes took place, and the Marathas were frequently hit by shells from the horse artillery.

There was, however, no advantageous result to either party. On 7 February General Smith entered Satara and captured the royal palace of the Marathas. He symbolically raised the British flag.

Bajirao II

On 19 February, General Smith got word that the Peshwa was headed for Pandharpur. General Smith's troops attacked the Peshwa at Ashti en route. During this battle, Gokhale died while defending the Peshwa from the British. The Raja of Satara was captured along with his brother and mother. The death of Gokhale and the skirmish at Ashti hastened the end of the war. By 10 April 1818, General Smith's forces had taken the forts of Sinhagad and Purandar. Mountstuart Elphinstone mentions the capture of Sinhagadh in his diary entry for 13 February 1818: "The garrison contained no Marathas, but consisted of 100 Arabs,

600 Gosains, and 400 Konkani. The Qiladar was a boy of eleven; the garrison was treated with great liberality; and, though there was much property and money in the place, the Qiladar was allowed to have whatever he claimed as his own."

On 3 June 1818 Baji Rao surrendered to the British and negotiated the sum of ₹ eight lakhs as annual maintenance. Baji Rao obtained promises from the British in favour of the Jagirdars, his family, the Brahmins, and religious institutions. The Peshwa was sent to Bithur near Kanpur. While the downfall and banishment of the Peshwa was mourned all over the Maratha Empire as a national defeat, the Peshwa contracted more marriages and spent his long life engaged in religious performances and excessive drinking.

12.3.2 Conflict with the Pindaris

The Pindaris, who were mostly cavalry armed with spears, came to be known as the *Shindeshahi* and the *Holkarshahi* after the patronage they received from the respective Maratha leaders. The major Pindari leaders were Chitu, Karim Khan, and Wasil Mohammad and their total strength was estimated at 33,000. The Pindaris frequently raided villages in Central India and it was thought that this region was being rapidly reduced to the condition of a desert because the peasants were unable to support themselves on the land. In 1815, 25,000 Pindaris entered the Madras Presidency and destroyed over 300 villages on the Coromandel coast. Other Pindari raids on British territory followed in 1816 and 1817 and therefore Francis Rawdon-Hastings wanted the Pindaris extinguished.

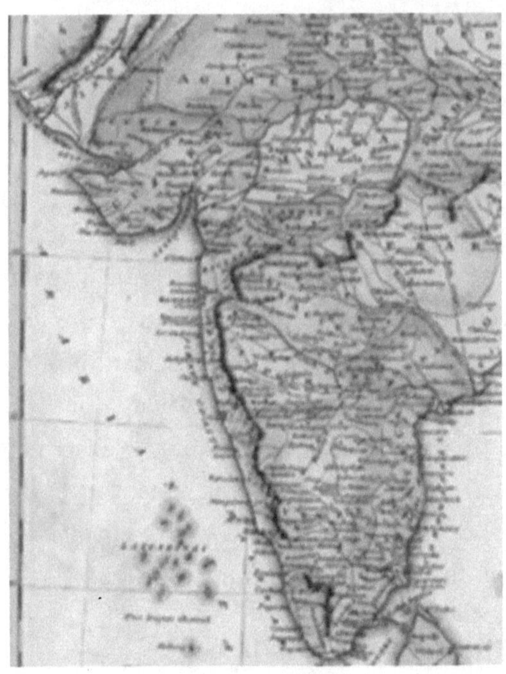

Location of Malwa in an 1823 depiction of India. Malwa was the headquarters of some of the Pindaris in the early 19th century

In opposition to what the British forces expected as they entered the region in late 1817, they found that the Pindaris had not devastated the area. In fact the British found a super-abundance of food and forage, especially grain, which added immensely to the security of their supplies. The Pindaris were attacked, and their homes were surrounded and destroyed. General Hislop from the Madras Residency attacked the Pindaris from the south and drove them beyond the Narmada river, where governor-general Francis Rawdon-Hastings was waiting with his army. With the principal routes from Central India being occupied by British detachments, the Pindari forces were completely broken up, scattered in the course of a single campaign. Being armed only with spears, they made no stand against the regular troops, and even in small bands they were unable to escape the ring of forces drawn around them.

The Pindari forces proved unable to counter the British and the Pindari chiefs were soon reduced to the condition of hunted outlaws. Karim and Chitu had still 23,000 soldiers between them but such a force was no match for the armies that surrounded them. In whatever direction they turned they were met by British forces; defeat followed defeat. Many fled to the jungles, while others sought refuge in the villages, but were killed without mercy by local villagers who had not forgotten the sufferings they had been inflicted upon by the Pindaris. All the leaders had surrendered before the end of February 1818 and the Pindari system and power was brought to a close. They were removed to Gorakhptir where they obtained grants of land for their subsistence. Karim Khan became a farmer on the small estate he received beyond the Ganges in Gorakpur. Wasil Mohammed attempted to escape, and after he was found Mohammed committed suicide by imbibing poison. Chitu, another Pindari warrior, was hunted by John Malcolm from place to place until he had no followers left. He vanished into the jungles of Central India in 1819 and was killed by a tiger.

12.3.3 Events in Nagpur

Mudhoji Bhonsle, also known as Appa Saheb, consolidated his power in Nagpur after the murder of his cousin, the imbecile ruler Parsoji Bhonsle, and entered into a treaty with the British on 27 May 1816. He ignored the request of the British Resident Jenkins to refrain from contact with Baji Rao II. Jenkins asked Appa Saheb to disband his growing concentration of troops and come to the residency, which he also refused to do. Appa Saheb openly declared support for the Peshwa, who was already fighting the British near Pune. As it was now clear that a battle was in the offing, Jenkins asked for reinforcements from nearby British East India Company troops. He already had about 1,500 men under Lieutenant-Colonel Hopentoun Scott. Jenkins sent word for Colonel Adams to march to Nagpur with his troops. Like other Maratha leaders, Appa Shaeb employed Arabs in his army. They were typically involved in holding fortresses. While they were known to be among the bravest of troops, they were not amenable to discipline and mostly armed with only matchlocks and swords. The total strength of the Marathas was about 18,000.

Sitabuldi Fort today

The British Residency was to the west of the Sitabuldi Fort located close to Nagpur. The British East India Company troops occupied the north end of the hillock associated with the fort. The Marathas, fighting with the Arabs, made good initial gains by charging up the hill and forcing the British to retreat to the south. British commanders began arriving with reinforcements: Lieutenant Colonel Rahan on 29 November, Major Pittman on 5 December, and Colonel Doveton on 12 December. The British counterattack was severe and Appa Saheb was forced to surrender. A force of 5,000 Arabs and Hindustanis however remained secured within the walls of Nagpur with the British laying siege to the city from 19 December. Attempts by the British to breach the walls failed with the loss of over 300 men, of which 24 were Europeans. The British agreed to pay the defenders 50,000 rupees to abandon Nagpur, which they did on 30 December. A treaty was signed on 9 January 1818. Appa Saheb was allowed to rule over nominal territories with several restrictions. Most of his territory, including the forts, was now controlled by the British. They built additional fortifications on Sitabuldi.

A few days later Appa Saheb was arrested. He was being escorted to Allahabad when he escaped to Punjab to seek refuge with the Sikhs. They turned him down and he was captured once again by the British near Jodhpur. Raja Mansingh of Jodhpur stood surety for him and he remained in Jodhpur, where he died on 15 July 1849 at 44 years of age.

12.3.4 Events in Holkar

The Court of Holkar, based at Indore, was at this time practically nonexistent. The dynasty was headed by 11-year-old Malhar Rao Holkar III under the regency of his dead father's mistress Tulsi Bai Holkar. Tulsi Bai was executed by her own troops in December 1817 for allying with the British; soon after, the British advanced into Holkar's territory, encountering his army about 40 km north of Indore at the Battle of Mahidpur.

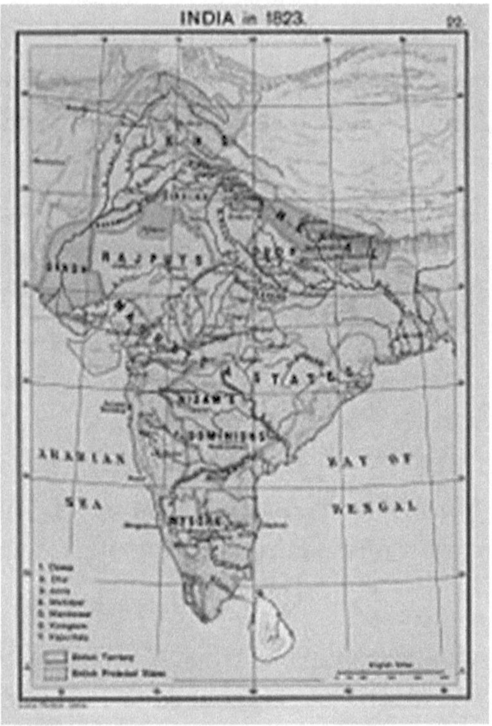

Map of India after the Third Anglo-Maratha War, 1819

The battle of Mahidpur between Holkar and the British was fought on 21 December 1817, lasting from midday until 3:00 am. Lieutenant General Thomas Hislop was commander of the British forces which came in sight of the Holkar army at about 9:00 am. The British lost around 800 men but Holkar's force was destroyed, with about 3,000 killed or wounded. These losses effectively knocked the Holkar out of the conflict and broke the power of the Holkar dynasty. The Battle of Mahidpur also proved to be a major setback for the Marathas as well. Henry Durand wrote, "After the battle of Mahidpur not only the Peshwa's but the real influence of the Mahratta States of Holkar and Shinde were dissolved and replaced by British supremacy." The remnants of Holkar's army were pursued across the territory by the British, suffering further casualties in small-scale skirmishes. Holkar was captured and his ministers made overtures of peace, and on 6 January 1818 the Treaty of Mandeswar was signed; Holkar accepted the British terms in totality. Large quantities of spoils of war was taken by the British, which remained an acrimonious issue for many years afterwards. Holkar came under British authority as a puppet prince subject to the advice of a British Resident.

12.4 Operations against remaining Maratha forces

By mid 1818, all of the Maratha leaders had surrendered to the British. Shinde and the Afghan Amir Khan were subdued by the use of diplomacy and pressure, which resulted in the Treaty of Gwailor on 5 November 1817. Under this treaty, Shinde surrendered Rajasthan to the British and agreed to help them fight the Pindaris. Amir Khan agreed to sell his guns to the British and received a land grant at Tonk in Rajputana. Holkar was defeated on 21 December 1817 and signed the Treaty of Mandeswar on 6 January 1818. Under this treaty the Holkar state became subsidiary to the British. The young Malhar Rao was raised to the throne. Bhonsle was defeated on 26 November 1817 and was captured but he escaped to live out his life in Jodhpur. The Peshwa surrendered on 3 June 1818 and was sent off to Bithur near Kanpur under the terms of the treaty signed on 3 June 1818. Of the Pindari leaders, Karim Khan surrendered to

Malcolm in February 1818; Wasim Mohammad surrendered to Shinde and eventually poisoned himself; and Setu was killed by a tiger.

Asirgarh Fort

During the last stages of the conflict, from 1818 to 1819, British military operations switch to capturing Maratha-held forts which were still holding out under the command of their qiladars. On February 27, 1818, British forces under the command of Sir Thomas Hislop approached Thalner Fort, assuming it was friendly; the fort's qilidar, Tulsiram Mama, ordered his troops to fire on the British, outraging Hislop who laid siege to the fort. After ordering several bombardments against the fort walls, he personally led a storming party which captured the fort and overwhelmed its garrison (which was comprised mostly of Arab soldiers). Mama was tried and executed for perfidy, and was hung on a nearby tree. Other forts in the region, such as Naralla Fort and Malegaon Fort were gradually captured and occupied by the British. At Malegaon Fort, the British encountered unexpectedly strong resistance from the fort garrison, which led them to bring in a 2,600-strong reinforcement force consisting of a mixture of infantry and artillery, after which a storming party captured the fort.

In early 1819, almost all of the forts had been taken, with the lone holdout being Asirgarh Fort, which was under the command of qiladar Jeswant Rao Lar. In March of that year, a massive British contingent lay siege to Asirgarh, capturing and occupying the town next to the fort to serve as a temporary base of operations. The 1,200-strong garrison was subject to constant artillery bombardments before the British launched an assault, which led to the fort's capture on 9 April. With the capture of Asirgarh Fort, the British victory was complete and all military operations ceased.

12.5 End of the war and its effects

The war left the British, under the auspices of the British East India Company, in control of virtually all of present-day India south of the Sutlej River, either through direct British rule, or through princely states. The famed Nassak Diamond was seized by the Company as part of the spoils of the war. The British acquired large chunks of territory from the Maratha Empire and in effect put an end to their most dynamic opposition. The terms of surrender Malcolm offered to the Peshwa were controversial amongst the British for being too liberal: The Peshwa was offered a luxurious life near Kanpur and given a pension of about 80,000 pounds. A comparison was drawn with Napoleon, who was confined to a small rock in the south Atlantic and given a small sum for his maintenance. Trimbakji Dengale was captured after the war and was sent to the fortress of Chunarin Bengal where he spent the rest of his life. With all active resistance over, John Malcolm played a prominent part in capturing and pacifying the remaining fugitives.

The Nassak Diamond was seized from the Peshwa by the British and sent to London

The Peshwa's territories were absorbed into the Bombay Presidency and the territory seized from the Pindaris became the Central Provinces of British India. The princes of Rajputana became symbolic feudal lords who accepted the British as the paramount power. Thus Francis Rawdon-Hastings redrew the map of India to a state which remained more or less unaltered until the time of Lord Dalhousie. The British brought an obscure descendant of Shivaji, the founder of the Maratha Empire, to be the ceremonial head of the Maratha Confederacy to replace the seat of the Peshwa. An infant from the Holkar family was appointed as the ruler of Nagpur under British guardianship. The Peshwa adopted a son, Nana Sahib, who went on to be one of the leaders of the Rebellion of 1857. After 1818, Mountstuart Elphinstone reorganized the administrative divisions for revenue collection, thus reducing the importance of the Patil, the Deshmukh, and the Deshpande.

The new government felt a need to communicate with the local Marathi-speaking population; Elphinstone pursued a policy of planned standardization of the Marathi language in the Bombay Presidency starting after 1820.